A Fourth Naturalist's Guide
to Lakeland Waterfalls
throughout the year

Mary Welsh

First Published 1989

ISBN 0 902272 80 2

© Westmorland Gazette

Published by
Westmorland Gazette,
22 Stricklandgate, Kendal, Cumbria

Printed by
Titus Wilson & Son Ltd, Kendal, Cumbria

A Fourth Naturalist's Guide to Lakeland Waterfalls throughout the year

By Mary Welsh

Illustrations by David Macaulay

Contents

Map Number	Waterfall	Page Number
1	Waterfalls on Black Combe, Whitbeck	9
2	Birker Force, Eskdale	14
3	Waterfall in Red Gill, near Eskdale Green . . .	19
4	Waterfall on Pull Beck, between Hawkshead Hill and Skelwith Bridge	23
5	Spout Force, Darling How Plantation, below Whinlatter Pass	28
6	Waterfalls in the grounds of Brantwood, Coniston Water .	34
7	Greenburn Waterfalls, below Great Carrs . . .	39
8	Waterfalls in Far Easedale, Grasmere	44
9	Waterfall on Tarn beck, below Seathwaite Tarn, Dunnerdale	49
10	Waterfalls in Swarthbeck Gill, Ullswater . . .	54
11	Waterfalls on Torver Beck, near Coniston . . .	60
12	Waterfalls in Mere Gill, below High Seat, Thirlmere .	65
13	Waterfalls on Newlands Beck, Newlands . . .	71

Contents *(Continued)*

Map Number	Waterfall	Page Number
14	Waterfalls in Roughten Gill, Blencathra	77
15	Moss Force, Newlands Hause	82
16	Waterfalls in Meg's Gill, Chapel Stile	87
17	Waterfalls on Over Beck, west of Yewbarrow, Wast Water	92
18	Waterfalls in Mill Gill, Great Dodd, Vale of St. John	98
19	Waterfalls on Far Ruddy Beck, Crummock Water	104
20	Waterfall, Warnscale Bottom, below Haystacks	110
21	Waterfall above Browney Gill, Great Langdale	115
22	Waterfalls above Ellers Beck, Maiden Moor, Derwent Water	120
23	Waterfall in Whelpside Gill, Thirlmere	125
24	Waterfalls in Wray Gill, Grasmere	130
25	Waterfalls between Helvellyn Screes and Whelp Side, Thirlmere	135
26	Waterfall in Blindtarn Gill, Silver How, Grasmere	140

Book Four

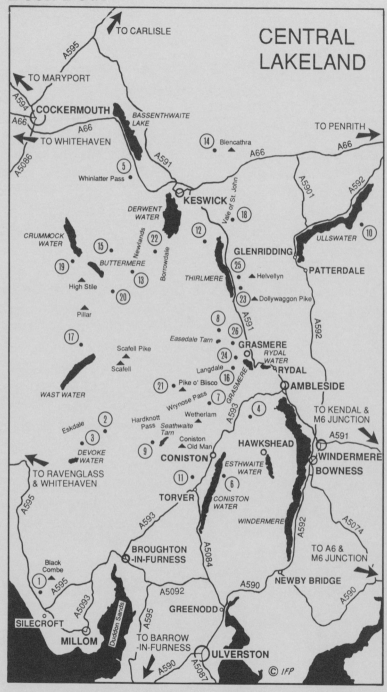

CENTRAL
LAKELAND

Foreword

This, the last of my four books on Lakeland's waterfalls, covers walks which, for reasons of space, were omitted from the previous volumes. In it, as in the other three books, I have guided the walker along the best routes to some of the loveliest falls in this delectable part of England. The book starts with walks in January and procedes through the year describing the weather encountered and the plants and birds most likely to be seen.

It has been a great joy to visit these glorious, hidden beauties of Cumbria. I hope this volume and the other three waterfall books have encouraged, and will continue to encourage, those fellwalkers who find the tops and the very long climbs rather daunting.

I have received much encouragement to complete this series by good folk who, throughout the seasons, visit a waterfall each week. My family have helped greatly by often accompanying me on my happy wanderings in Lakeland. I am also grateful for the support given me by David Macaulay who has illustrated the last three books in the series with such sympathetic skill. Lastly I must mention my border collie Cammie who has walked with me on all my explorations and hopefully will continue to be my companion as I move over the border into Yorkshire in search of more waterfall walks.

Waterfalls on Black Combe, Whitbeck

Waterfalls on Black Combe, Whitbeck

E arly in January the day can dawn with the sky suffused with red, but a lowering greyness can follow rapidly. If the day before has been bitterly cold then the grey clouds will be heavy with snow. There is only time for a short, brisk walk to waterfalls not too far into the fells and not too high up into the icy winds.

Park in the lay-by at St. Mary's church on the A595 at Whitbeck between Millom and Bootle. The church, a single storeyed building sitting above the main road, is quiet and peaceful inside with the Christmas crib just beyond the entrance door. Look at the visitors' book started in 1937, with its many interesting entries.

St. Mary's Church

After leaving the church take the road that leads up towards the fell. Along the verge, dandelions and groundsel are still in bloom and the leaves of wild parsley and foxglove are a bright green. A buzzard sits very still, hunched on a field post and a male blackbird with glossy black feathers and a bright-yellow bill feeds ravenously on the still-profuse crop of rose hips. In a nearby pasture rooks and gulls are searching for insects where cattle have trampled and softened the ground. Several redwings with pale eyestripes and reddish sides settle on a sycamore hedge and then fly off with a strong, direct flight.

Blackbird and rose hips

Beside the road is a tumbling beck. A low hedge beyond shelters wrens, chaffinches, robins and a mistle thrush. Follow the lane as it swings to the left and leads to a cattle grid. Oak, ash and hazel break the force of the cold wind. Beyond the grid take a wide track that goes off to the right over the fell. Just before it swings down to the beck and the waterfalls, the walker can glimpse the snowy top of Black Combe at the head of the gill.

Continue along the path as it bears to the right and to the base of three charming waterfalls. The beck makes a steep drop in a wide fall of water and then divides into two streams to fall into a pool. The water separates once more into two long jets which unite to race over its rocky bed. The white-topped water tumbles again in two long foaming falls which plummet to a wide, flat-topped outcrop of rock. And still its joyous leaping is not finished, for very soon the stream divides into three. One flow of water slides down a narrow gully, the other two leap exuberantly over a precipitous rock face to fall in long, long white tresses of water which speedily join with the side stream to tumble on down the gill.

Here one can find liverwort, fern, moss, heather and gorse, the latter covered with yellow flowers. Here too is shelter from the searching wind and shelter for the patient sheep.

Return along the beck side to the path and walk past an old mill. Look at the huge wooden water wheel on its far side and a row of fine beeches that protect the mill from the worst of the gale. Further on the path becomes wide and grassy and crosses the fell. Away to the left is the sea, dull grey like the sky. To the right the fell slopes are a rich brown now that the bracken is dead.

Between the sea and the path are farm pastures and, in one of the meadows,

Sheltering sheep and flowering gorse.

fieldfares with slate-grey heads probe the soil for food. Soon the walker comes to several small quarries that have been used in the past for collecting stone for buildings. Beyond these the path becomes fully exposed to the freezing wind and, as a few snowflakes begin to fall, it is time to return. This is a pleasant walk for a very cold January day.

O.S. Map SD119847
miles

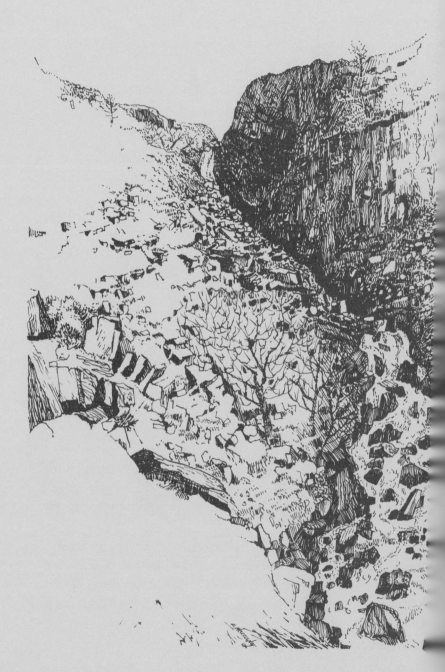

Birker Force, Eskdale

I n late January, when gales blow fiercely along the coast, the walker will find a gentle quietness in the valley of the River Esk. Park in Trough House car park and continue along the track beyond the park, following the directions for Birker Fell. Pass through two gates and, after walking a short distance along the bridlepath, take a gate on the left signposted Boot and Upper Eskdale. This track leads to the bottom of Birker Force, one of many superb waterfalls in this lovely vale.

To the left of the path is a walled wood with a mixture of oak and conifer. Just over the wall is a pool with large concentric circles forming on its surface caused by continual drops of rainwater seeping out of the thick coating of moss that covers the trunk and most of the branches of an ancient oak.

Follow the path across a grassy meadow to a gate in the wall that gives access to a small wood of mature oaks. Through the trees race the waters that have tumbled so spectacularly through Stanley Gill. A wooden bridge enables the walker to cross dryshod. Below is a ford and remains of stepping stones which once were the only way for pedestrians to cross this turbulent beck. Here the calls of tree creepers are heard over the noise of the water and very soon the white of their breasts reveals them industriously searching the mossy trunks for prey. Great tits and blue tits pass through the branches overhead, they too engrossed in the never ending hunt for food.

A gate beyond the bridge opens onto an area of grass and dead bracken, surrounded by fine silver birch and overlooked by the austere, creviced faces of Hartley Crag and Gate Crag.

Continue walking ahead on a path that comes close to the fast flowing River Esk, magnificent after so much rain. Cross a small stream below a clump of oaks and head towards a row of stepping stones across the Esk. The path leads to the little church of St. Catherine standing alone among the pastures on the opposite bank. In the churchyard is an ornate tombstone engraved with the name of Tommy Dobson, the Eskdale huntsman, with the carved head of a fox on one side and a hound on the other. Today the stepping stones are under water.

Walk on along the river bank for nearly half a mile until the way is obstructed by a wall, then climb up the sloping bank to join a bridlepath that leads towards Birker Fell. A gate here opens onto a wide path, a pink band through green sward. The pink is soil formed from Eskdale granite that gives this valley its warm colouring. Gorse bushes, with a scattering of yellow blossoms, flourish and beyond these to the right stands a row of closely planted firs. These trees almost hide from view a lovely clear tarn that reflects the steep slopes above. Its sides are softened with yellowed sedge and, in a clump of fir, blue tits and goldfinches, with equal acrobatic grace, search for insects.

After enjoying this secluded tarn, return to the path and continue to a gate in a drystone wall. Through the bars of the gate can be seen the surging water of Low Birker Beck racing madly to join the Esk. The beck can be crossed by a deep ford but fortunately a narrow bridge has been built and the walker can keep his boots dry.

Follow the track as it skirts a fir plantation and at Low Birker

Farm take the right hand fork that leads up the fell. Beyond the first wall is a gate and a sheep trod leading to the bottom of the Force. Find a comfortable rock and look up at the astounding fall. It is a curtain of white water, narrow at first and then widening to a wall of foam. This great torrent drops steeply through the sheer-sided gill. Birch, rowan, sycamore and ash grow where they can but in late January their buds are tightly closed and all seems lifeless except for the lively, dancing water.

Return to the path that ascends the fell. In the last century the folk of Eskdale used this wide grassy peat track to bring down their fuel on sledges from the marshy slopes above. The path rises steeply among berry-laden juniper bushes to the fell wall. Once the walker is through a wooden kissing gate the old peat road zig-zags upward. Pause often on this arduous climb and enjoy the views of Scafell, Bow Fell and Crinkle Crags. Here the ubiquitous bracken is replaced with heather and an occasional larch.

Low Birker peat hut

And then the track strides across the rim of a plateau, past the Low Birker peat hut. Its sturdy walls have remained intact but, alas, the roof has gone. Where the track swings away to Low Birker Tarn and Green Crag, follow a short well-worn path to the top of the force. In a grassy sheltered dell, picnic beside a deep, brown pool. This is in constant motion, disturbed by the water

Cascades on the lower Birker Beck.

that has drained from the peaty plateau and Low Birker Tarn. It tumbles in white cascades into the brown pool and then leaves it by two foaming streams that hurtle along rocky slipways before leaping ecstatically to the valley bottom far below.

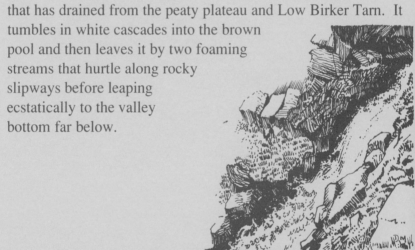

O.S. Map NY187999
4 miles

Rocky slipway where
the beck makes a water slid

*Waterfall in Red Gill,
near Eskdale Green*

Waterfall in Red Gill, near Eskdale Green

S ometimes February is heralded by fiercesome gales blowing from the east. These sweep over the snow-covered tops and carry hail and icy rain as they race out into the Irish Sea. On such a day the walker looks for a waterfall sheltered in a deep gill and such a place is Hare Gill, down which tumbles a delightful waterfall on its way to join the little beck joyously chattering through Red Gill.

There are several verge-side parking places close to the gill on the unfenced road between Ulpha and Eskdale Green but there is a larger parking area at the beginning of the farm road that leads to High Ground and is signposted Stanley Ghyll.

Walk down the narrow road towards Eskdale Green enjoying the panoramic view of the white-crowned Lakeland giants. Cross Black Beck, which hastens below the road in a flurry of white water. Then just beyond a very wet area take a sheeptrack on the left that leads down the fellside away from the road. The hardy fell sheep avoid the wettest areas and their tracks take one safely around the edge of any marsh. They also lead to shelter and this track is no exception, taking the walker into the quietness and seclusion of Red Gill.

Black Beck enters Red Gill in a series of pretty cascades that foam over water-blackened rocks, before dancing on through the steep sided ravine. The track keeps close to the beck, sometimes crossing to the other side when the way is impeded by a steep rock

Black Beck enters Red Gill in a series of pretty cascades

face. Huge boulders litter the slopes. Russet brown bracken and moss soften the outlines and rowan, birch and pine grow tall in this hidden valley, just below the road.

The beck that tumbles down Hare Gill topples in long white tresses until small ridges of rock stop its headlong rush, causing the beck to cascade. It then falls in another long white wall of water in a tremendous hurry to join Black Beck in its race to reach the River Esk.

Climb the right side of the gill. The sheep track sets off up the fell from beneath a graceful rowan and leads to the top of the waterfall. From here the narrow beck can be seen idling across the marshy fell to the edge of its first fall. Birch, with deep red branches and buds, cradle it all the way down its reckless leap. Cross the beck and follow the track past holly, rowan and birch, as it slopes downhill to the side of the beck once more.

21

Return to the road and walk back towards Ulpha. Here beside the road, in drainage ditches cut through the rich peaty soil, hard fern grows abundantly, a deep green against the brown water and bleached mat grass. When the road begins to climb steeply take a wide cart track off to the left that crosses the fell and comes close to the walls of High Ground.

Yellow hammer

A pair of yellow hammers shelter from the fierce wind perched close to the top stones of the wall. The male is resplendent in its nuptial plumage, its head much brighter than the lichen on the nearby stones. Close by, its browner mate is almost prostrate against the rock. Both stay a long time enjoying the warmth of the intermittent February sunshine.

At the end of the track turn right and walk along the farm road to return to the parking space.

Hard fern

O.S.Map SD165987
2^1/2 miles

Waterfall on Pull Beck, between Hawkshead Hill and Skelwith Bridge

Waterfall on Pull Beck, between Hawkshead Hill and Skelwith Bridge

Park the car just beyond Sunny Brow. For motorists travelling from Coniston the car park lies on the left side of the road. A footpath sign beside the road alerts one to the small parking space and from here a wide path leads through a sheltered valley to the base of Pull Scar and the fall, now frozen after a sharp spell of icy weather.

Follow the path beside a deep beck where water mint leaves glow bright green beneath thick ice. Pass through another gate beneath a pollarded ash and continue along the edge of a larch plantation. Sycamores have been used here as nurse trees for the young larches. From among the trees a green woodpecker announces its presence with its familiar laugh or 'yaffle'.

Among the larches and above on the open fell foxhounds are excitedly sniffing the ground and racing hither and thither searching for a trace of their quarry. A huntsman in traditional pink blows his horn calling sternly to the lively dogs.

Where yew and gorse come close to the edge of the path a pair of bullfinches fly across a small clearing between the shrubs, flashing their square white rump patches. Their black heads, stubby bills and the pinky-red breast of the male show clearly in the light of a brilliantly sunny March day. Here, hazel catkins are now quite long.

Further along, huge larches with long pendulous branches loaded with cones lean gracefully over the path. Beneath are

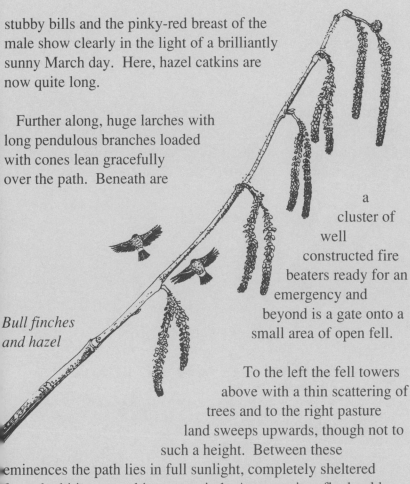

Bull finches and hazel

a cluster of well constructed fire beaters ready for an emergency and beyond is a gate onto a small area of open fell.

To the left the fell towers above with a thin scattering of trees and to the right pasture land sweeps upwards, though not to such a height. Between these eminences the path lies in full sunlight, completely sheltered from the biting, searching east wind. A convenient flat boulder encourages one to sit and enjoy the sun and watch a jay sunning too. It flies off across the clearing, its white rump, blue and black speculum and glowing breast ready for its nuptials.

Very soon the path joins a bridlepath. Follow this to a gate and a stile. Ahead in the distance lies the Fairfield Round, a huge white mass against a duck-egg blue sky. Below, Lake Windermere is now edged with ice. Over the drystone wall that has bordered the right side of the path for much of the walk a

25

lapwing calls plaintively and a snipe rises from the pasture and flies off.

The path leads down through silver birches, their trunks almost white in the sunlight. These are soon replaced by mature beech whose long pointed buds are just beginning to swell. Ahead lies a gate to the road but do not take it. Cross the little beck to the left of the path and go through the woodland to the edge of the Pull Beck.

Climb up the bed if you enjoy a scramble and the conditions are right, or keep along the top of the gill with the tumbling beck below. A few hundred yards brings one to the foot of the fall.

Pull Beck, a long white streak of ice, snakes down from Pull Scar, passing through the ancient trees that clothe the lower slopes. It falls over a sheer drop into a hollow at the head of the steep-sided, narrow gill. On the almost perpendicular slopes grow beech, larch, oak and holly with ivy sinuously covering many trunks. A party of long-tailed tits hunt for insects in the top of an oak, high up in the sunshine, undisturbed by a pair of ravens flying towards rocks on the scree far above. The sides of the gill are covered with a rich loam and, where small depressions provide flatter areas, bronze beech and oak leaves pile up. A redwing, disturbed, flies off showing the orange-red patch under each wing. The beck flows strongly under a layer of ice. Moss covering rocks is stiff with frost, wood sorrel leaves are dark green and limp, and liverworts isolated from the spray by the ice are black and

Ivy

shrivelled. The fall immediately ahead has been transformed into a huge chandelier of ice, riveting the attention. The beck's long drop has been fixed in thousands of sparkling icicles, each one glistening in the sunlight. Here and there the light is split and all the colours of the spectrum are revealed.

Pull Beck frozen

Beneath the beck's silvery, frozen face the water continues to fall and its happy chattering fills the secluded gill. The steep sides of the gill keep out the searching wind but not the bright sun which, in spite of its warmth, has not thawed the silvery spears.

With care it is possible to clamber close enough to examine this icy wonder. At the top is a tier of short icicles, beneath are mounds of fluffy ice. Below this again is a tier of much longer ice spears, with more hummocks of ice piled one on top of the other. Towards the bottom is yet a third tier of icicles with huge mounds of clear ice filling the base of the hollow.

A drumming is heard and a great spotted woodpecker is seen pecking at the rotten branch of an oak. The eye is caught by the brilliant crimson patch under its tail and on its nape and its black and white garb. Eye-catching too are the leaves of the honeysuckle, the sun shining through their young greenness.

O.S. Map NY346016
3 miles

Spout Force, Darling How Plantation, below Whinlatter Pass

L eave the A66 by the B5292 to Braithwaite. Drive through the village and continue up the road as it climbs towards the pass. Vast plantations of conifers stretch away on either side, but close to the road deciduous trees grow and the vegetation is lush and verdant. Four miles beyond Braithwaite look for the signpost on the right-hand side of the road giving the direction for Spout Force. Turn right into the farm road and park in a small lay-by a few yards along. Overhead flies a crow with what looks like a large rodent in its bill. It flies slowly, continually moving the position of its prey as the plump small beast struggles to escape. The corvid then circles over the conifers and descends out of sight, presumably to a mate incubating a clutch of eggs.

Climb the stile and walk diagonally across the pastures to the yellow-banded trail marker post. Pass through a gap in a broken wall at the extreme tip of a spur of Darling How Plantation and continue to the next marker post. This stands close to a stile that gives access to the plantation itself, with another marker post seen between the trees just inside the forest. A man-made, muddy path leads down the very steep hillside among the straight, sweet smelling trunks of spruce. The dark umbrella of

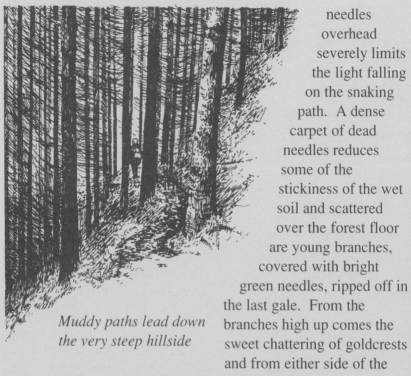

needles overhead severely limits the light falling on the snaking path. A dense carpet of dead needles reduces some of the stickiness of the wet soil and scattered over the forest floor are young branches, covered with bright green needles, ripped off in the last gale. From the branches high up comes the sweet chattering of goldcrests and from either side of the path can be heard the rushing of water as small becks hasten downhill.

Muddy paths lead down the very steep hillside

At the bottom of the steep slope the path emerges from the trees and continues to the edge of Aiken Beck. This lively stream winds its way along the narrow valley through acres of conifers that stretch steeply upwards, the topmost trees lost in swirling mist. Away to the left lies Scawgill Bridge, carrying the road to Cockermouth. The trail lies over a wooden footbridge ahead and then, indistinct but clearly marked, moves into the forest, always keeping in sight or sound of the brook. Coltsfoot flower at the water's edge and coal tits fill the valley with their conspiratorial whisperings.

The path climbs higher and deeper into the trees where foxgloves with rosettes of fresh young leaves colonise the rocky

outcrops. Continue walking straight ahead to
a railed viewing point overlooking the lovely
Spout Force. The Aiken flows quite leisurely
to the edge of the precipice and then leaps
tempestuously into the yawning chasm. At
first it cascades, dallying momentarily about
some rocky projections, before dropping in a very long, wide
curtain of white water. It falls into a seething pool almost hidden
by a wall of rock, then swirls through a narrow gap into another
basin of boiling foam. From here it surges on over its rocky bed
in the narrow valley.

Several ash trees, starkly white against the backdrop of
conifers, stand at the head of the waterfall. All are heavily
garlanded with moss, lichen and polypody ferns. Spleenwort and
more polypody festoon the many-coloured layered shale. Great
banks of liverworts luxuriate in the constant spray from the
outermost streamers of water that ricochet off the confining sides
of the ravine. A grey wagtail, head and neck dipping at every
step, moves sedately over spray-drenched mossy flats. Suddenly
it runs nimbly after a dancing mosquito and it is lost to sight
because its slate-grey back exactly matches the wet rocks. It
turns and reveals its sulphur-yellow underparts
in full breeding finery.

Continue along the path that winds
through the plantation, passing
above the falls, before
dropping down to a wide
cleared area beside the
beck. Here
among the
decaying
tree
stumps

Frogspawn in pool

31

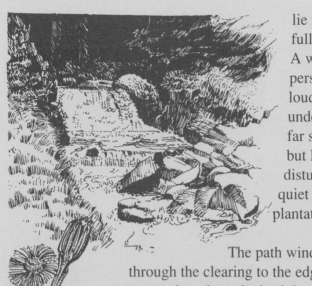

lie many tiny pools full of frog-spawn. A wren sings persistently and loudly from undergrowth on the far side of the beck but little else disturbs the intense quiet of the extensive plantation.

The path winds its way through the clearing to the edge of a series of pretty cascades where the beck leaves a narrow canyon and conifer crowns tangle overhead. Climb the path, moving up into the trees away from the beck. Follow it as it passes through a compartment of larch where the extra light has transformed the forest floor into a brilliant green carpet of grass, moss and wood sorrel. To one side the forest drops very steeply to the silvery beck far below.

When the path comes to a forest road turn right and walk to the main track a hundred yards ahead. Turn right and walk past Darling How Farm to return to the start of the walk. A small diversion to the right leads to a railed area overlooking the forest clearing with its pools and frog-spawn. Further on a forest ride leads sharply downhill to another fenced area just above the falls.

Small upper fall and coltsfoot

Unfortunately the splendour of the falls is hidden from sight but there are delightful glimpses of the layered shale and its many plants.

).S. Map NY182260
? miles

Waterfalls in the grounds of Brantwood, Coniston Water

Brantwood, the home of John Ruskin for more than a quarter of a century, lies on the eastern shore of Coniston Water. This charming house, with its magnificent view, can be approached by a narrow road from either Coniston or Ulverston, or by boat across the lake. Whichever route to the house is taken it enhances the pleasure of a visit to this quiet Lakeland backwater. There is ample free parking space below the house, and inexpensive tickets for the three-and-three-quarter mile nature trail that meanders beside all the waterfalls can be obtained from the main entrance.

Take the steep steps to the right of the entrance and follow the yellow arrows that clearly mark the route for the whole of the walk. Pause at the numbered stops and look around. A trail guide obtained with the ticket explains what to see at each stop. The first part of the walk, along narrow paths through woodland, was a favourite haunt of Ruskin's. In early April, the slopes on either side of the path are a mass of daffodils lighting even the darkest parts where rhododendrons crowd out the light and western red cedar and western hemlock tower into a misty grey sky. Pale pink azaleas and snowdrops bloom together and the rich green leaves of bluebells foretell a later blossoming. Goldcrests 'si,si,si' in the evergreens, chaffinches sing, finishing each song with an exuberant ending, great tits call their sweeter song of

April and the flute-like melody of blackbirds seems to come from every bush. Through the trees on the right Coniston Water gently laps its stony shore.

The trail leaves the confines of the trees by a kissing gate and crosses a meadow. A stile gives access to another woodland area. Here hazel catkins sway in the breeze, dog's mercury is in flower and the leaves of wild arum have unrolled. A green woodpecker is disturbed and flies out of the trees and across the open land with its easy, bounding flight. Once through a gap in the wall walk to the right, to the corner of the field, to view an old bloomery that lies beside the tumbling Beck Leven. Beneath the clump of trees by the heap of slag and cinder wild strawberry leaves cover the ground. Walk back up beside the stream and enjoy the first of the foam-topped falls as the beck hastens on its way to lose its energy in the lake. A stile in the wall ahead leads into more woodland where various species of moss carpet the ground. Coal tits move quickly through the trees hunting for insects and chuckle conspiratorially to each other as they go.

Dog's mercury

As the sun comes out it catches the sparkling water racing through the ravine to the right of the path. Continue climbing gently through the trees taking care when viewing the falls in the gorge below. Ferns, mosses and rushes cover the steep sides wherever they can maintain a hold and the lushness of this great cleft contrasts sharply with the woodland all around where spring has not yet arrived. Further along the path, to the right, a graceful waterfall descends through the leafless trees in three raging jets. Walk on beside the beck which is soon joined by another that falls in chuckling tumbles. More bluebell leaves have emerged and some of the dead trees support large, leathery discs of bracket fungus. By the stile at the end of the wood the beck descends in more cascades.

Out on the open fell, away from the protection of the trees, the full force of the easterly wind is felt. Dead leaves are picked up and whirled across the pasture. Herdwick sheep huddle against the wall. Pass through the gate above and turn left, keeping beside the wall. From here the lake lies far below, silvery and still. Beyond, its grandeur veiled in mist, is the Old Man, its gullies white with snow. Turn right up the fell, following the path to Crag Head, which is bordered with dead heather and bleached grass. From the cairn on the top enjoy the splendid view of the lake with the houses of Coniston village hugging its shore. Birch, holly and juniper grow sparsely on the top and meadow pipits flit across the vegetation but there is no sign of nuptial flights as yet.

The well defined path now heads downhill across open fell to a stile leading into woodland. Here another small beck rages through a steep gorge and there are more attractive falls, to be viewed with care. The path drops gently down the slopes between larch festooned with pink 'roses' and sycamore with fat green buds. Wood

Bracket fungi

sorrel leaves and moschatel grow in dampish patches. Continue along the path as it once more winds between huge banks of rhododendrons until the house appears through trees on the right. A short distance ahead and another small waterfall is reached. Just beyond the fall stands Ruskin's seat, an armchair of slate. Here the famous man would sit, with his

Ruskin's Chair

back to the marvellous view across the water and the mountains beyond, and enjoy the impetuosity of the little beck racing beneath a shadowing elm. He would have enjoyed the water as it is today, racing between birch, holly and rhododendrons, tangling with a huge clump of spurge glowing golden in the thin afternoon sun.

Ruskin's Waterfall

O.S. Map SD312954
SD312957

4 miles

Greenburn Waterfalls,
below Great Carrs

Greenburn Waterfalls, below Great Carrs

A fter some quick refreshment at the Three Shires, Little Langdale, walk down the narrow lane just beyond the hotel. This is signposted Tilberthwaite and leads to the River Brathay. The lane is bordered with hazels laden with catkins but as yet there are no leaves, even though it is the end of April. Chaffinches abound in the cottage gardens.

Having walked a hundred yards or so look for a kissing gate on the right that gives access to the pastures beyond the lane and is signposted Slaters Bridge. Oak, ash and thorn bushes straggle over the ground and a great spotted woodpecker flies off as it is disturbed. Ahead are the snow covered tops.

Slaters Bridge

The track leads to a ladder stile and then drops downhill to the lovely Slaters Bridge across the Brathay. After heavy rain the river surges in a great rush beneath the intricate stonework. To the right is Little Langdale Tarn, flooded, with both trees and sedge submerged. It is from here that the racing water issues. A pair of mallards are busy in a small backwater, well out of the hurrying mainstream.

A recently-born lamb bleats piteously and approaches three ewes in turn, only to be butted away. And then from some distance its mother hurries across to it and it suckles contentedly.

Lowest falls

Follow the track to some throughs in the wall ahead. These lead to a lane. Turn right and walk along the lane overtopped on one side by huge heaps of slate waste. The lane passes some cottages and beyond these the mound of slate continues, with nature having little success at colonising it. An odd birch and rowan and a small patch of moss is all that is visible from the lane.

Pass High Hallgarth and its cypress beyond, to a gate across the track. Ahead is the open fell and a wonderful vista of the Langdale Pikes still topped with snow. The near fellside is noisy with the sound of falling water as many tiny becks tumble down in a great hurry to Greenburn Beck below. This wide, foaming beck is bordered with birch. As the racing water flows, impeded by boulders, it turns a beautiful shade of turquoise and then foams onwards to add to the flooded tarn.

Where the path divides take the left fork, and enjoy a magnificent view of the angry Greenburn Beck. In the distance the road over Wrynose Pass winds up the fellside. Meadow pipits ascend and descend and flit across the path that climbs beside the beck - a good path generally, but a very wet one after several hours of rain. To the left, the beck in Birk Fell Gill races downhill, crossing the path before joining the major beck. The wind catches the lovely waterfall high on Birk Fell, whipping the water into the air, causing a tiny fountain and a vast cloud of spray.

At the next gate is the first view of the spectacular, foaming waterfalls as the Greenburn Beck leaves the disused reservoir high in the hills. A pair of ravens fly across the blue sky and an occasional cloud causes the sunlight to race across the bleached slopes of Hollin Crag.

The lowest fall is a huge mass of foam as the beck races around rocks and rages against boulders in its path. At the fall above, the water piles up in fury unable to get through a narrow gap in the rocks. White water froths and boils, and spray is tossed high and then caught by the biting wind.

In a hollow beside the next highest waterfall is a turquoise pool sheltered from the searching wind, its surface still and undisturbed. Below the roaring fall a protruding boulder divides the water, which surges sullenly until it joins again before entering a small ravine. Here rowan, alder and holly grow and meadow pipits cavort.

Top waterfall

The path continues beside the beck and then passes through a derelict coppermine, which still has some walls, doorways and bridges intact. To the right of the mine the Greenburn makes its most ecstatic leap. White jets hurtle down steep slopes then circumvent thwarting boulders. It rages on in a wall of white water. Once through the disused mine the path, indistinct now, crosses a flattish area covered with very wet sphagnum and clubmoss. A drystone wall to the right supports a causeway that runs beside the Greenburn Reservoir, now disused. Here is the place to eat one's sandwiches, close to the water and yet sheltered by boulders from the icy blasts that cause the water to ripple and surge. These down-draughts come from the surrounding snow-covered mountains. Wetherlam lies to the left, with snow on its top and down its gullies.

The reservoir receives its water from the slopes above and from the highest reaches of Great Carrs, the lofty mountain that stands sentinel-like and snow-crowned at the head of Greenburn Valley.

O.S. Map NY286023
5 miles

Waterfalls in Far Easedale, Grasmere

A walk to waterfalls that starts in Grasmere is always a joy. The village is busy and full of interesting shops, and sometimes it is difficult to tear oneself away. After a quick browse in the bookshop leave the car in the small car park in Easedale Road, then walk on along the road. A notice beside the gate across the road confirms that vehicles can go no further. Beyond the gate the road continues between wide, grassy verges where marsh marigolds, buttercups and dandelions flourish.

From the oaks and sycamores that crowd the lower skirts of Helm Crag a cuckoo calls. Where the track appears to divide, follow the signpost for Far Easedale. Wild cress grows in the marshy areas beside the track and a blackbird sings strongly. Away to the left Sourmilk Gill waterfall, visited in Book One, descends in a great mass of white foam.

The road now deteriorates into a track and a gate ahead gives way to a wide path through a wood of birch and sycamore. Another signpost directs the walker towards Far Easedale. Here the path is bordered with larch and beech and here too robins and wrens sing and scold. Near the farm on the left-hand side of the track are pollarded oak and ash. Above to the right rooks are busy flying from fell to tree-top nests and a pheasant crows.

By an old barn on the right is a walled pasture in which grows a splendid monkey puzzle tree, a huge spruce and a larch. Here too a cuckoo calls regularly. The path becomes a stony stairway rising steeply between high walls. Climbing it must have been hard work for the pack ponies who regularly journeyed with heavy burdens between Grasmere and Borrowdale many years ago. Today it taxes only the walkers enjoying Far Easedale or using it as a pass over the fells to the youth hostel in Borrowdale.

And then the beck is reached; a lovely, chattering beck that gurgles over its stony bed with many a white flurry, and passes between banks lined with young fern, ash, rowan and birch. A yellow hammer calls from the depths of a hawthorn. The path climbs beside the beck through open fell to a quiet valley. As the land becomes flatter so the beck flows more gently and all is tranquil.

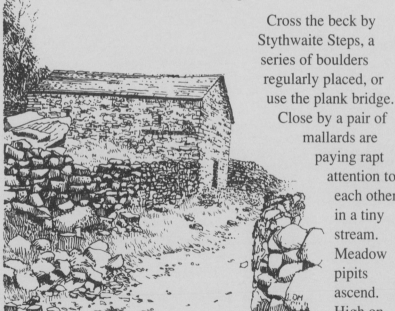

Barn, Far Easedale

Cross the beck by Stythwaite Steps, a series of boulders regularly placed, or use the plank bridge. Close by a pair of mallards are paying rapt attention to each other in a tiny stream. Meadow pipits ascend. High on the rocky

Ring ouzel

slopes to the right are juniper bushes and scattered over the fell are hawthorn.

Once a sheepfold on the far right of the path is passed, leave the path and cross to the beck, now racing through a narrow rock cutting. Where liverworts and wood anemones thrive, the beck makes a dramatic descent in one continuous fall of foaming water before it races through a steep-sided canyon.

Return to the path and climb gently. Away to the right the beck makes another sharp descent in a number of pretty cascades, the water white-topped as it hurries over numerous rock ledges. After crossing a small side stream recross the fell to the side of the beck where it tumbles yet again, in tresses of white over water-blackened rocks. Here in a crevice, below the lichen-covered boulders scattered over the fell, grows parsley fern, bright green and delicately leaved. Along the edge of the water rowan, ash and birch mingle with holly and juniper.

The beck now ambles gently across the fell, making wide arcs as it goes. The path, though rocky, rises gently. In a marshy area, fat, lively tadpoles swim, enjoying the warmth of the sun. A black beetle hurries across the path and a wireworm wriggles over the soil between the boulders. Above to the right are the crags of Pike of Carrs and to the left are the towering heights of

Three splashing falls

Deer Bields. From the latter comes the continuous screeching of young peregrine, pleading to be fed. On the lower slopes of Deer Bields a ring ousel calls regularly, a clear, piping call, unworried by the peregrine family above.

The beck is noisy now as it tumbles down steeper slopes. Then the lovely lower cascades are reached. Three splashing falls tumble one after the other through young fern, bracken, wood sorrel, moss and violet. Beneath a shadowing rowan bilberry grows, laden with pretty bell-shaped flowers.

Clamber up beside the beck to where a stream that has risen on Moor Moss tumbles in a long, charming waterfall to join the main beck. The two watercourses plunge over stepped rocks to converge and flow along a narrow chasm under rowan and juniper. Here beside the lively, dancing water untamed by narrow gorges, fissures or boulders, the walker may sit and think and look back down this lovely valley of Far Easedale.

O.S. Map NY302099
6 miles

*Waterfall on Tarn
Beck, below Seathwaite Tarn,
Dunnerdale*

49

Waterfall on Tarn Beck, below Seathwaite Tarn, Dunnerdale

T he lane from Duddon Bridge leading to Seathwaite is lined with spring flowers and bushes laden with blossom in the last week of May. Here abound bluebell, herb robert, ramsom, dandelion, primrose, shirt button, cow parsley, wood sorrel, celandine, violet, yellow poppy, milkmaid and dock, together with young bracken and lush grass, making the verges the very epitome of an English spring. In the hedgerows are blackthorn, flowering late this year, May, wild cherry, bird cherry, and oak with a mass of tiny green flowers. A male bullfinch flits from one side of the road to the other. Pairs of swallows sit on wires in front of the eaves of each

Oak in flower

farmhouse along the valley and house martins dart overhead.

Park on the grass verge before the second cattle grid after leaving the village of Seathwaite. Just below, to the left, lies the River Duddon, noisily making its way seaward. Above, on its far bank, the fellside is a patchwork of greens. The dark green of Scots pine and cypress contrasts sharply with the pale green of the beech, sycamore and rowan. Oak is still a yellow-green and the leaves of the birch are a half-tone greener. Regular outcrops of grey rock complete the charm of Dunnerdale Forest.

On the wall by the cattle grid a grey wagtail sits. Its back is grey-brown, with bright yellow above its tail and on its breast. Its beak, needle-sharp and black, opens and closes rapidly as it calls incessantly. It flies into the air after an insect and then, with wings outstretched, it parachutes back onto the wall curving its tail upwards as it alights.

Grey wagtail catches an insect.

Walk back a few paces along the way you have come and then take a wide, tractor-rutted track on the left that winds on between Troutal Tongue and High Tongue. Wheatears flit ahead and the wetter areas are covered with low-growing sedge, now in flower. Dow Crag shadows the valley beyond, and away to the far left is the first sighting of the waterfall, hidden from the road by the Tongues and Brow Side. The path rises and as the walker comes to the brow the noise of the falling water can just be heard. Climb the stone steps in a wall from where the Walna Scar road, White Pike, Brown Pike, Buck Pike and Dow Crag can all be seen.

The path drops now and passes through a birch plantation where wood sorrel flowers, bracken croziers push through last year's dead fronds and a scrub willow has tiny catkins but as yet no leaves. Beneath a huge oak, resplendent in its new foliage, pass through a gap in a small wall that leads to the edge of Tarn Beck. Here a green woodpecker calls loudly, willow warblers sing constantly and a pair of robins scold, anxious for the safety of their brood in the wall.

Follow the path through this lovely, sheltered, sunny wood following the current of the beck. Enjoy the warmth and the tree pipit's repetitive, plaintive notes as it settles in the tree tops. When a gap in the fell wall is reached follow the path in an arc to drop down the fell, diagonally, to a gap - a 'fat man's agony' - in the wall below. Beyond, where wood anemones and pale pink violets grow, turn left and follow the wall round to a gated, wooden bridge across the beck. A brightly feathered yellow hammer sits in the hazel along the waterside and cheerfully serenades the sun.

Turn left and walk back along the beck to a gate onto the road, continuing through Tongue House Farm where more yellow hammers flit between pastures and the hedge lining the beck. Here a muddy track leads out onto the fell where moorland crowfoot fills peaty pools. Keep to the track, for the ground around can be very wet, and cross a stile and then a ladder stile over the next two walls. Pass through a gap in the next wall and

it is but a short walk
to the foot of the
lovely fall tumbling
down the fell from
Seathwaite Tarn.

Long white foaming
streams of water race pell-
mell down the fell, finding
their route where they can, as
huge boulders bar their way.
The sparkling, dancing water
encircles small islands, where
rowan, birch, willow and oak are
covered with delicate leaves and where,
by contrast, juniper and holly are sombrely clad,
and ash is still in bud. In hidden hollows, through
which the lively beck hastens, grows honeysuckle
laden with leaves. And beneath this trailer thrive
moss and liverwort, bracken and fern, all lush and very green.

*Wood
anemone*

Beside this charming, secluded fall is the place for a picnic and
a siesta. Then, refreshed, cross the falls with care and head for
the ladder stile on the brow. More violets and celandines grow
around the stile, wheatears and yellow hammers haunt the rocks
and walls and the noise of the falling water is all around.

Follow the path a third of the way down the fell and then take a
gate on the left to cross diagonally to the farmhouse below.
From here it is a short walk along the path to the car.

*O.S. Map SD240985
3 miles*

Waterfalls in Swarthbeck Gill, Ullswater

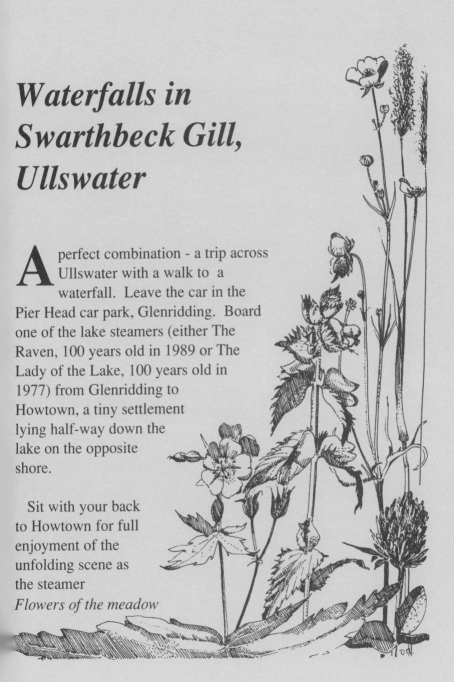

A perfect combination - a trip across Ullswater with a walk to a waterfall. Leave the car in the Pier Head car park, Glenridding. Board one of the lake steamers (either The Raven, 100 years old in 1989 or The Lady of the Lake, 100 years old in 1977) from Glenridding to Howtown, a tiny settlement lying half-way down the lake on the opposite shore.

Sit with your back to Howtown for full enjoyment of the unfolding scene as the steamer

Flowers of the meadow

progresses. Peak and high ridge seem to crowd the view ahead, misty, lofty and seemingly unattainable. Small islands float serenely, lapped by a gently wash from the few boats allowed on this peaceful lake. Notice the wooded slopes of Birk Fell unfold where birch and juniper almost reach the top. Look for Scalehow Force (visited in Book 3) racing down the hillside and marvel at the brilliant colour of the mass of broom growing on the slopes of Gowbarrow Park.

Disembark at the tiny pier, turn left and walk past a glorious hay meadow, riotously colourful with buttercup, pink clover, meadow cranesbill, yellow rattle, lady's bedstraw, bird's-eye, crosswort, common sorrel and meadow grass. Twenty yards further on look for a signpost poorly placed just beyond the entrance to Howtown Outdoor Centre showing the way to Pooley Bridge. Cross the field ahead, past a spectacular clump of wild balsam, following white-topped posts directing the walker to a gate, some steps and a second gate on the right. Turn left to follow a lovely high-level walk above the lake.

Walk on along this wide grassy path where yellow hammers sing from the walls, wheatears scold and pied wagtails pause, wary of approaching their young while intruders are about. Meadow pipits abound, perching on large rocks or soaring into the warm air, and young rooks, black beaked, feed in the pastures below. Continue on for three-quarters-of-a-mile to the bridge at the foot of Swarthbeck Gill. Below the bridge the silvery beck races through a densely wooded area where a green woodpecker calls.

Climb up the right-hand side of the beck. The gill goes up exceedingly steeply, littered with huge boulders for all its length. The vegetation is luxuriant; parsley fern, male fern, lady fern, golden saxifrage, mossy saxifrage, violets and tormentil cover the

Rowan roots and rocks

ground, grow in crevices or ring the necklace of pools that stretch down this rocky ladder. Little shade is cast by the trees and bushes growing on the far side of the gill - hawthorn, covered with white blossom, rowan equally and attractively burdened, berried holly, elm and birch.

It is a stiff climb to the dog-leg bend in the gill but beyond lies a pleasant, flattish area where one can ease aching legs. Walk to the bottom of the lowest cascade, where the sun catches each droplet of water as the beck races around a huge moss-covered boulder. Look up through the vegetation to a foaming rock slide and higher still to a long jet of water that furiously finds its way through a narrow crevice in an impeding boulder. About this secluded hollow grow large mats of alpine lady's mantle. Listen to the cuckoo calling from the valley below and enjoy the view of Blencathra, dark and forbidding on the horizon.

For many walkers this will be the point of return, back to the path above the lake to catch the afternoon steamer back to Glenridding. For those who wish to continue, the way up the gill lies along narrow sheep tracks and high above the exceedingly steep sides that slope down to the beck. It calls for a cool nerve

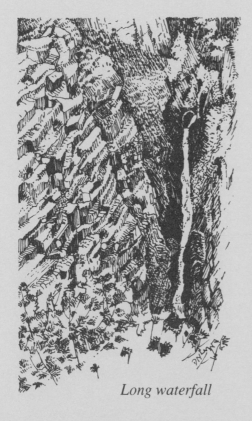
Long waterfall

and a sure eye and foot. Walkers continue at their own risk to view the lovely waterfalls ahead.

Cross the beck and follow a zig-zag path that leads upwards to a promontory from which the falls viewed earlier can be seen again. Scramble on up to another promontory where a foaming fall descends beneath ash and rowan. With care continue upwards until you can stand steadily to enjoy a magnificent fall that plummets forty feet or more. Look for the planes in the bedding rock on the opposite side of the beck, each line catching the glorious sunshine. Follow the indistinct path, ever upwards, until a deep hollow lies at one's feet and there again is another beautiful fall. A well-worn sheep track enables the walker to walk round the rim of the hollow and, beyond, the beck can be seen idling through the bottom of the gill.

From here strike up the very steep slopes to the top of the ridge where fell ponies graze and sometimes frolic in the sun. Keep well away from the edge of the rocky crags overlooking the lake and head towards the fascinating cairns on Bonscale Pike. Walk along the top of the ridge, enjoying the magnificent views over the Lakeland fells with Scotland in the distance until the Fusedale

Beck comes into view far below. The views need to be savoured long and enjoyed with the ravens whose territory the walker now shares.

The path across these upper fells is narrow but well defined. Follow it when it begins to slope steeply downwards towards Mellguards. It is a long way to the bottom of the valley and again one's leg muscles yearn for relief before the descent is over. If there is time, turn left and walk through Mellguards and Howtown, past more hay meadows, and sit on the little beach watching for the steamer to ply its way up the lake from Pooley Bridge. Here you might see a pair of red-breasted mergansers snoozing on the gently lapping water.

).S. Map NY455205
°¹/₂ miles

Waterfalls on Torver Beck, near Coniston

High summer, and the lanes leading to Little Arrow, Torver, are magnificent. Foxgloves, meadow sweet and dog daisies fill the verges with colour. Bramble, elderberry, dog roses and honeysuckle perfume the hedgerows and please the eye with their luxuriance. Each cable carrying electricity to the farms along the way has its brood of tiny swallows, balancing precariously because of their still very short tail feathers. Attentive parents attempt to assuage their hunger, chattering noisily meanwhile. Greenfinches and goldfinches serenade the summer morning and a kestrel hovers unusually high above.

Park in a lay-by in front of the houses that make up this small hamlet. Follow the signposted direction between the cottages to a gate that gives access to a sturdy path that climbs the fell. Bracken now dominates much of the slopes but in wetter areas marsh thistle, spearwort and forget-me-not grow. In very wet areas, where bracken cannot maintain a hold, the ground is covered with purple orchis, contrasting sharply in colour with cotton grass, now a mass of woolly heads.

Oak, ash, hazel and holly are scattered across the fell which echoes with the songs of willow warblers, tits, chaffinches and robins. A great spotted woodpecker flies across a clearing among the trees and is lost to sight as it enters its hole in an ancient oak.

As the path swings up through the bracken, gorse bushes laden with a large crop of pods border the edges, and beneath these grow tormentil and self heal. Continue along the path, from which it is now possible to hear the Torver Beck tumbling rapturously downhill, hidden deep in its wooded gill. A small stream crosses the path and along its marshy sides grow bog asphodel, orchis, lousewort and spearwort.

Gorse with seed pods

Now the path is walled on both sides but the beck still fills the air with the noise of tumbling water. Beyond the next gate the walls are replaced by a row of scrubby hawthorn which hosts meadow pipits and yellow hammers, and the path is wide and of springy turf. Once past a barn and through another gate the walker comes to the edge of Torver Beck. Turn left along the side of the beck, first climbing beneath a large alder, then ascend a small slope to a sheep trod through the bracken that leads to a grassy promontory.

From here look back along the beck to where it drops in four lovely cascades, one after the other, white topped as projecting boulders thwart its passage. After rushing though a deepish pool the water slides in a flurry of spray in four small jets over a steep wedge of rock to fall into another dark pool before chattering on its way. Here the beck is shadowed by beech, oak, ash, rowan, birch and alder. In the shade of these trees grow bracken, polypody, yellow pimpernel, cow-wheat and marsh bedstraw. A large crop of hawkweed, each flower a golden yellow, appears to bring the sun into the deep shade of this secluded silvan scene. These flowers grow on the steep slopes of the gill, on the floor of the wood and wherever there is a damp area, creating a warm glow of colour.

After this pleasant detour, return to the path and walk on, passing through an open gate with a ladder stile beside it. Bear left along a track where shoulder-high bracken hides the dancing beck but does not dim its cheery noise. Very shortly this track rejoins the main path and leads to the base of a huge spoil-heap of slate. Follow paths that lead to the far left of the heap and then turn right, again skirting the base of this huge mound of spoil. Here among the cleverly laid stones of the retaining walls, spleenwort fern thrives.

Continue climbing, following the course of the beck. Close by a young greenfinch finds it difficult to cope with a large larva it has found and immature wheatears, in fledgeling down, look larger than their attentive parents. A pair of spotted flycatchers adroitly catch insects, then return to the same perch or another favoured branch.

Fungi on ash

The path through the bracken, near to the beck, now rises steeply and from the slopes dozens of meadow pipits rise into the warm summer air, trilling continually, then parachute downwards still carolling. Just before the immediate brow is reached walk right through the bracken to the water's edge.

  As one clambers downhill there are good views of the waterfall. The beck leaves Goats Water and gently idles across a wide marshy area before leaping down the steep slopes into the gill. It cascades white topped over boulders and drops in foaming jets between banks lined with ash and birch. Its sparkling water splashes bracken, polypody, bilberry, tomentil, foxglove, thyme, moss and wavy hair grass alike. Sit on a large boulder in mid-stream and look up at this charming fall and enjoy its impetuosity as it hastens on its way towards Coniston Water.

First fall in shady woodland

O.S. Map SD273965
3^1/$_2$ miles

Waterfalls in Mere Gill, below High Street, Thirlmere

Waterfalls in Mere Gill, below High Seat, Thirlmere

North of Thirlmere the A591 becomes a dual carriageway for just over half-a-mile. Where the road continues as three lanes, a bend in the old route to Keswick has been by-passed to avoid a dangerous corner. The old road has been left as a lay-by and the north end provides convenient parking for the walk to the waterfalls in Mere Gill.

Walk back to the edge of the beck and pass through the gap on the right in the drystone wall. Follow the track beside the beck to the gap in the wall ahead. Cross the A591 with care and walk

Chestn

along the lane ahead which leads to Shoulthwaite Farm. The lane keeps close beside the noisy beck, which lies deep in its rich high-summer vegetation. Horsechestnut, elm, ash, hazel and field roses, heavily laden with creamy flowers, hide the racing water. The verges of the lane are bordered with crosswort, kidney and tufted vetch, nipplewort, white and pink clover, dog daisies and hedge woundwort.

Where the lane swings left to the farm, look for a gate and a stile straight ahead. Look too for the spotted flycatcher that uses a bare branch of holly and the wire fence as a launching post to catch insects for its hungry brood. Beside a sign is a white arrow and the words "permissive path" which leads to a stile in the fell wall at the far side of the meadow. Beyond is a track through the foxgloves and bracken and beneath the large thrusting fronds the delicate climbing corydalis clambers.

This track joins a well defined path that continues left beside Shoulthwaite Beck. After much overnight rain the beck is in spate and a great torrent of peat-stained water surges downhill. It angrily descends the steep slope to the farm in a series of dramatic waterfalls beneath several large European larches. Their long, gracefully-curving branches burdened with numerous cones hang over the raging water. The track climbs steadily beside the lovely falls until the flatter ground above is reached. Bracken no longer dominates and the turf is colourful with self heal, eyebright, lady's mantle, bedstraw and marsh thistle. Tiny moths flutter over the flowers. Where small streams hurry to join the main beck, tom thumb, spearwort, biting stonecrop and forget-me-nots grow. On the far side of the beck conifers stretch upwards to the tops and down the far slopes to the shore of Thirlmere.

The path continues beyond a sturdy ladder-stile over the wall. Here the beck surges through two low walls forming a small weir. Overhead, blue tits industriously seek for insects among the tiny tassels of silver birch that edge the conifer forest, their chucklings very faint against the noise of the lively beck. To the right, high on Goat Crag, a long white fall of water slashes the grey rockside and in the air currents a raven displays to its mate perched placidly on a boulder. Continue along the path, which keeps in sight of Shoulthwaite Beck. Large boulders scattered over the fell provide convenient perches for young, speckled-breasted wheatears. Meadow pipits pipe plaintively but no longer rise ecstatically trilling into the air as they did a few weeks earlier. Another two waterfalls race down more crags to the right of the path and, where these streams cross the path to reach the Shoulthwaite, large mats of sundew, now in flower, grow among the sphagnum. Lousewort and butterwort thrive here too, but in the drier parts sweet smelling thyme covers the ground with a purple carpet.

Below Iron Crag the path traverses the scree that covers much of the slopes. On grassy islands among a sea of boulders sheep and lambs feed. On the other side of the beck the dense conifers are overtopped by Sippling Crag whose slopes and flats are covered with more evergreens. In birches that line the beck a grey wagtail scolds as the walker approaches its nest. It continues flying upstream, alighting regularly, spreading and raising its tail, a sharp angry call pin-pointing its perch on boulder or branch. The turbulent stream descends this lovely, secluded valley in foaming cascades and roaring falls, with much to satisfy a dipper that races into the hurrying water seeking food for its brood. Look back from here at the lovely vale of Keswick stretching away to the lower slopes of Skiddaw to the left and Blencathra to the right. Between them is the gently curving valley of the Glenderaterra.

Soulthwaite Beck

Continue deeper into the valley, which becomes narrower and the slopes on either side steeper. To the left is Castle Crag covered with bilberry, tall grass, foxglove and bracken with birch and rowan barely maintaining a hold. A drystone wall runs down from the crag to the left bank of the Shoulthwaite which tumbles down in foaming peat-stained jets below the site of an ancient fort. Under the lowest fall, in a dank hollow lined with liverwort, ferns and golden rod, it is joined by the beck that has descended Mere Gill - the object of the walk. The path comes to the edge of Mere Gill and, with care, climb up the slope beside the beck. Sit on a boulder just beyond the start of the wire fence and enjoy the splendid double fall that plummets downwards into a deep, boiling pool.

Continue climbing well away from the edge of the steep-sided gill until a higher path is reached. Return along this to the edge of the water once more. Cross the beck on boulders, slippery if the beck is in spate, to a flat, grassy hollow on the opposite bank. Above, down the steep narrow gill, the foaming, roaring, white-topped beck seems to come from the blue sky. The near-vertical fall of water splashes luxuriant ferns, golden rod, wood sage, foxgloves, thyme and heather as it plummets beneath rowan, ash, hazel and juniper casting its spray on bilberry now in fruit. It angrily rages round huge boulders into deep pools before it swings to the left in a white-topped jet and descends in yet

another jet that causes the pool at its base to be in constant turmoil. Beyond this pool it flows sedately past the grassy hollow allowing the walker to cross to the other bank before it drops again in the elegant double fall seen lower down.

The Soulthwaite Beck angrily descends the steep slope

O.S. Map NY298188
3 miles

Waterfall on Newlands Beck, Newlands

Waterfalls on Newlands Beck, Newlands

P ark by Chapel Bridge in the Newlands Valley or drive towards Little Town and make use of one of the several lay-bys between the bridge and the small hamlet. Take the gated mine road that leads south into the valley of Newlands Beck. To the left of the path bracken densely covers the steep slopes of Knott End and between the ubiquitous fern grow tormentil, foxgloves and bedstraw. To the right, beyond the beck, lies Scope End with its splendid conical shape seemingly detached from Hindscarth, of which it is the northernmost flank. Far to the right the top of Causey Pike is veiled in mist.

The old mine road makes for easy walking into the quiet isolated valley. A yellow

Scope End

hammer sings plaintively from the top of the wall beside the track. Others announce their presence in scrubby hawthorns scattered sparingly over the rock-strewn slopes. High above young buzzards screech, demanding to be fed. One of the adult pair circles above High Crags harried by a tiresome raven that would send it on its way.

Cattle graze around Low Snab Farm, which lies on the far side of the beck. A meadow close by the road supports a glorious array of summer flowers - wild parsley, buttercups, dog daisies and great burnet mingle with many species of grasses, their heads now heavy with seed. A slate sign in the wall advertises that pots of tea can be obtained at the farm across the bridge - something to be enjoyed on the return walk?

Behind the farm the brow of Scope End is riven with a deep gash, the upper pan-holes of Goldscope Mine. Here, in times gone by, silver and gold were extracted. Over the desolate piles of mine waste, house martins wheel, chasing flies that are attracted by the

Grasses in flower

73

cattle in the pastures below. Beyond the farm the track comes closer to the clear, fast-running stream. Where the latter makes a large meander the track rises high above the water as it races over its pebbly bed. Numerous speckled immature wheatears, now quite confident in their ability to fly, flit ahead and scold from the safety of scattered boulders. Meadow pipits, less obviously, call sweetly and quietly from the depths of this secluded valley.

After heavy rain the day before, the slopes resound to the falling of water as fast-flowing torrents descend in great haste to join the Newlands Beck. In the wet pastures beside the track where the hurrying water crosses the route, large patches of the lovely, delicate starry saxifrage grow. Several tall Scots pine shade a small cottage beside the path, named on the O.S. map as a climbing hut.

As the walker continues along the track the way ahead appears blocked by a huge, heather-clad crag. This is Castle Nook and over to the right is the large mass of Hindscarth. Below, in the valley bottom, the furious Newlands Beck descends in white-topped cascades. Follow the track as it winds

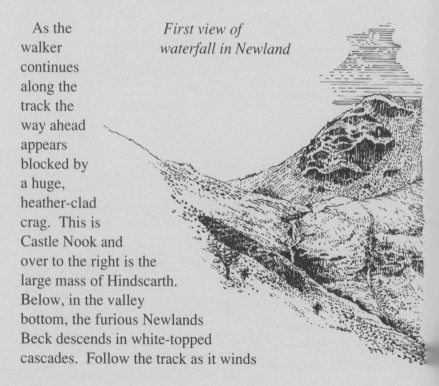

First view of waterfall in Newland

around the base of Castle Nook and there ahead lies the object of the walk - the splendid waterfall set in a dark hollow in the centre of an amphitheatre of steep grassy slopes and sheer crags with skirts of scree.

Just beyond Castle Nook, where the path divides, take the left fork which leads uphill into the quiet fells. The path is now choked with rocks and many boulders litter the ground. This appears a bleak vista at first sight but as the walker moves along the track past a solitary larch and into the rough terrain, many lovely plants are revealed. Parsley fern, hard fern and bristle fern fill the shady crannies beneath the boulders. Low growing bilberry covers the turf among the rocks with sweet smelling thyme, tormentil, hawkweek, harebells, bedstraw, buttercups, white clover and foxgloves providing bright touches of colour. In the wet areas starry saxifrage, eyebright, marsh thistle, yellow mountain saxifrage and sundew flower close together.

As the track climbs a ridge that runs down towards the magnificent waterfall, alpine lady's mantle covered with a profusion of flowers turn the mountain floor to pale yellow. Tiny red toadstools nestle among these lemon-coloured blossoms. Climb carefully down the ridge for the best view of the Newland's tempestuous leap past banks aglow with golden hawkweed. It flows through a deep, narrow gill, and rages white topped along a rock slide before surging round a giant of a boulder athwart its bed. It slews to the left beneath rowan, the water steely-grey, before dropping into a boiling pool. It cascades for a short distance, swirling into a small cave on its far bank. Then it is channelled through a narrow gap in the confining rock walls and the water builds up into a roaring, angry torrent before it falls in a glorious, wide, lace-like curtain of water. It drops for many feet, sparkling against a black walled hollow, toppling onto a ledge near the bottom of its tremendous fall and then raging on into a shallow basin at its base. Smaller falls slash the slopes of Hindscarth but none shows such turbulence as this foaming torrent.

Return to the track above the fall and follow a faint path, well defined by cairns, which passes close to the beck that descends in more cascades above the fall. Among the rocks beside the path stag's horn clubmoss grows and higher up rowans graciously clothe the sides of a small ravine. A grey wagtail flies upwards from a boulder in mid-stream and runs nimbly over turf close by the path, chasing a luckless fly. It regularly flicks its long tail revealing lovely ochre-coloured under feathers as it runs into a clump of alpine lady's mantle and is lost to sight.

Follow the trod beside the beck, past junipers that hug the boulders close to the water, until a marshy plateau is reached. Here lesser clubmoss thrives. Where the path comes to the edge of another little beck that drains higher ground beyond, cross over on rocks. Then step across the main beck and sit on an outcrop of rocks nearby and enjoy Dalehead Tarn which lies in a secluded hollow in the mountains. Sedge, which covers almost half of this small tarn, sways and bends in the wind that sweeps across the surface. Around the edge grow horsetail and these, too, caught in the strong breeze, bow and touch the water.

Pause here awhile before making a decision on which way to go back. Return either by High Spy - unless you are discouraged by the steep slope which is not nearly as steep as it seems and is a marvellous high-level walk - or take the seemingly less arduous route back through Newlands Valley. Both routes provide breath-taking views of Keswick and Skiddaw.

O.S. Map NY229161
5¹/₂ miles

Waterfalls in Roughten Gill, Blencathra

Waterfalls in Roughten Gill, Blencathra

T wo delightful waterfalls lie hidden in Roughten Gill, a deep cleft in the side of Blencathra. Visit these in late July when the fells ring to the song of pipits and wheatears, and the turf is spangled with tormentil and bedstraw.

Leave the A66 at the signpost for Threlkeld. In the centre of the village take the steep turn up the fell that passes the school and leads to the Blencathra Centre. Here the tarmac ends and a wide track continues to a small parking area. Beyond, the track skirts the steep slopes of Blease Fell, climbing gently, giving the walker a delightful view over Derwent Water to the north-west peaks, with wisps of mist about their tops. Dew still lies trapped among the sheeps' wool scattered on the ground and a greenfinch sings cheerily from an oak.

Follow the path as it bears to the right. Far below is the Glenderaterra Beck, sparkling in the sunshine. On the other side of the valley is Lonscale Fell, with its sharp peak and steeply inclined scree slopes running down to the old mine below on the bank of the beck.

The path runs close to a pretty fall tumbling down from Blease Fell. The foaming water falls over rock steps covered with bright green moss and liverwort. A rowan, covered with tiny green

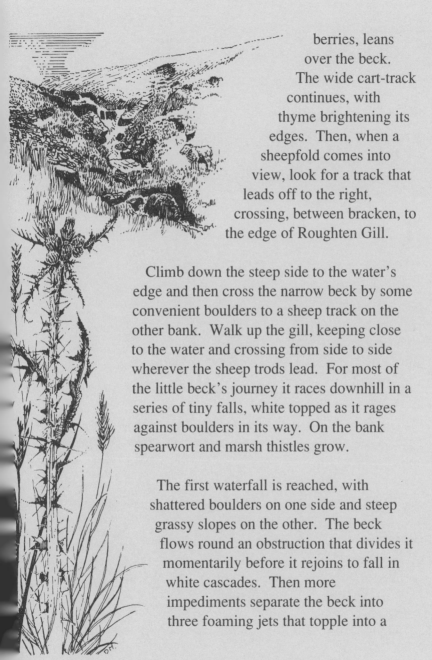

berries, leans
over the beck.
The wide cart-track
continues, with
thyme brightening its
edges. Then, when a
sheepfold comes into
view, look for a track that
leads off to the right,
crossing, between bracken, to
the edge of Roughten Gill.

Climb down the steep side to the water's
edge and then cross the narrow beck by some
convenient boulders to a sheep track on the
other bank. Walk up the gill, keeping close
to the water and crossing from side to side
wherever the sheep trods lead. For most of
the little beck's journey it races downhill in a
series of tiny falls, white topped as it rages
against boulders in its way. On the bank
spearwort and marsh thistles grow.

The first waterfall is reached, with
shattered boulders on one side and steep
grassy slopes on the other. The beck
flows round an obstruction that divides it
momentarily before it rejoins to fall in
white cascades. Then more
impediments separate the beck into
three foaming jets that topple into a

ower falls with marsh thistle, sedge and sheeps fescue

deep pool. After tumbling down three large rocky steps it topples into yet another pool before racing on down the gill.

Continue walking through the gill. Under boulders close to the water's edge grows parsley fern, with bright dark-green leaves. Here too grows polypody, bedstraw, fescue and sedge.

Very soon the top waterfall is seen, dropping in a long white plume of water over a steep cleft between closely confining rock walls. It races down a rock ladder, foaming wildly as it bounces off each step. Finally it falls into a pool in a sheltered hollow before surging on. Stand on the edge of the hollow and enjoy the species-rich vegetation. Heather, now in flower, hangs over the fall, shadowed by a rowan. Rush, moss, bilberry, spearwort, liverwort and bracken fill every 'rock garden', luxuriating in the spray. Bright yellow hawkbit grows in great profusion as if bringing sunshine into the depths of the hollow.

This is a charming fall, surrounded by much vegetation and adorned with so many shades of green. Part of its attraction is the unexpected

Upper falls

lushness hidden in a fold of the stark slopes of Blencathra.

To return, strike up the right-hand slope above the beck until a sheep trod is gained at about 2000 feet, and then follow it southwards. From here there is a magnificent view of the Pennines, blue and distant; of the Solway and the mountains beyond; of Derwent Water with Keswick on its shore; of Borrowdale and the Jaws richly clad in trees; of Thirlmere like a jewel surrounded by its pines; of Helvellyn free of cloud at last, standing giant-like above High and Low Rigg, with Tewet Tarn a tiny patch of blue; and lastly, like a small necklace set on a green cloth, is the circle of stones at Castlerigg.

Keep at the same height until the main path is reached. This leads down the rocky slopes and then through bracken to the car park.

).S. Map NY305277
NY309279
miles

Moss Force, Newlands Hause

The drive from Braithwaite to Newlands Hause is a delightful way to approach the waterfall. The steep slopes of Barrow and Causey Pike to the north, and Cat Bells and High Snab Bank to the south, give this road through the hills a charm of its own. The towering mass of Robinson lies at the head of the pass and as the car climbs to the highest part of the Hause, Moss Force is seen to its best advantage. In sight of the tumbling water and just above the brow of the hill are two convenient verges for leaving the car. Here too is a persistent sheep approaching every car for food - much to the irritation of the dog which has endured a long ride in order to enjoy a very long run on the fells.

This dramatic fall of water tumbles in a great long white jet through a narrow, steep-sided cleft down the crags at the base of Robinson, where it borders the Hause. First it drops in a racing stream from a dip in the top of the crags. Where several rowan trees maintain a precarious hold, a large boulder divides the water and it rages on as two thin jets. After uniting it flows along a rocky slipway to hurtle down and down through the steep gully into a pool. Here juncus, hawkweed, heather, tormentil, bed-straw, butterwort, bracken, polypody, parsley fern and the lovely mountain fern all thrive in the spray.

Climb the path and then take a narrow track through the bracken to a hollow by the edge of the force from where there is a glorious view of the beck on its journey down the remainder of the gill passing more rowans as it goes. Ahead it can be seen winding through the valley, keeping close to the road, on its way to join the Keskadale Beck.

Return to the main path and climb the very steep slopes that border the force's steep cleft. Many feet have taken the same route and in places the path is badly eroded. At the top, turn right and continue along the track, through juncus, with bedstraw and tormentil scattered among the rush. Crummock Water and Loweswater lie far below sparkling in the sunshine, and on looking back Derwent Water stretches away towards the northern fells. In time the path meets the footpath that comes up from the village of Buttermere.

The path now bears round to the left, skirting Buttermere Moss, a very wet area indeed. Keep to the path as it winds its way through bog asphodel and tormentil, taking advantage of every drier area. Do not stray into the patches of pale green woolly hair moss as they hold large quantities of water. The Moss is the territory of pipits and wheatears and the air is filled with

Bog asphodel

their songs. Pipits ascend and chase each other over the rocky outcrops. Wheatears perch and scold on nearby boulders, warning the dog not to get too close to their broods.

Once across the Moss the path ascends towards the summit of Robinson. Skiddaw slate, shattered into small pieces, litters the track, a way that is steep and requires care in climbing. It is well cairned and, from half way up, Buttermere is seen, deep blue in its rock basin.

Wheatear

View fom Robinson

At last the summit of Robinson is reached, a flat rock-strewn plateau where little grass can grow. There are cairns around the edge of the plateau from which the best views can be obtained. The largest cairn is the highest point. The views are breath-taking, comprising the Solway and its mountains beyond, Great Gable, Green Gable, Scafell Pike and its acolytes, and Helvellyn.

O.S. Map NY194174
3 miles

Waterfall in Meg's Gill, Chapel Stile

Waterfalls in Meg's Gill, Chapel Stile

A t last the walk to the waterfalls in Meg's Gill, Chapel Stile. In mid-August the journey around the edge of the deep gully is very enjoyable and quite safe, unlike the first attempt in Book One, when the glory of the falls remained hidden because the track was deep in snow.

Leave the car close to the wall in the lane leading to the church. Walk past the church and the houses to where a little beck falls down the fellside, on the left, by a drystone wall. It passes noisily beneath oak, ash and rowan.

The path to the waterfall climbs steeply, keeping close to the beck. It is a distinct path through the bracken and round huge boulders. Foxgloves, tormentil, heather and wild thyme flower wherever they can find a space. Huge layers of slate are exposed where the path crosses a stream and dragonflies dart across the splashing water in the warm afternoon sun.

Rest awhile when a small plateau is reached and appreciate bog asphodel, spearwort and mossy saxifrage while you catch your breath.

Continue climbing, keeping close to the wall where bird's foot trefoil grows and a wren scolds from nearby bracken. The path

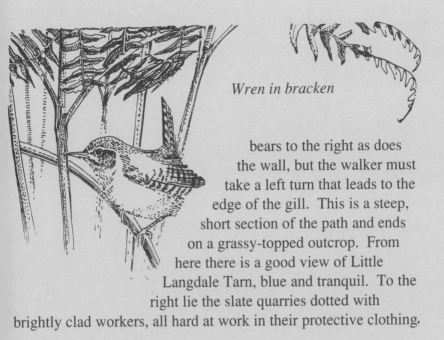

Wren in bracken

bears to the right as does the wall, but the walker must take a left turn that leads to the edge of the gill. This is a steep, short section of the path and ends on a grassy-topped outcrop. From here there is a good view of Little Langdale Tarn, blue and tranquil. To the right lie the slate quarries dotted with brightly clad workers, all hard at work in their protective clothing.

The track now passes through low bracken, near to the steep sides of the gill. Below lies the beck winding between oak and birch. Then the track moves away from the gill edge and becomes a wide grassy swathe through the ubiquitous bracken. It ends where another small stream crosses the path and where spearwort grows in profusion. Beyond this the way becomes eroded, a brown gash on the fellside. From a solitary hawthorn a robin 'ticks' angrily and eventually flies further away from tiresome intruders of its peace. Stand by the hawthorn and look back. Windermere lies in the far distance surrounded by its gently wooded slopes and walled pastures. In the quietness of Meg's Gill the waterfalls, though unseen, suddenly and noisily make their nearness known.

A few more steps up lead to a desolate rocky flatness and to the place where the main beck comes down from the left through crags, rocks and scree. To the right the racing water drops over a ledge and is lost to sight. With care the walker can peer over this lip of rock and see the falling water, tumbling down and down, under rowan and birch, between juniper, heather and foxgloves heavy with flowers.

Cross the beck and follow the path to the right, round the head of the gill. Within a few steps, stop and look back to where the waterfall is revealed in all its glory. The track runs close to the edge and crosses a few yards of scree, but a pause is essential as the view deserves to be savoured slowly and at length. After its first short fall, the water slides over a broad rock face in tresses of white to fall into a shallow pool. It makes another short drop before it descends in a white curtain beneath a rowan bright with red berries.

The narrow track leads away from the edge to a cairn and the waterfalls are lost to sight, but not for long. The cairn marks the ridge route and this should be followed to the east, crossing the top of Spedding Crag. From here the beauty of the waterfall can be seen once more from the top, where it slips over the ledge of rock, to where the beck becomes a sparkling, silvery band in the gill bottom.

From the ridge route there is another wonderful

Spearwort, thyme and harebell

iew, this time of Grasmere and Dunmail Raise to the left and ydal Water to the right. Above the lake rises the grassy ounded mass of Fairfield. Rydal Beck, foam-topped, lies in the epths of the horseshoe-shaped range.

After fifteen minutes of gentle walking leave the ridge path for track striking off to the right through the bracken. Keep earing towards the right as the path swings round under the heer, smooth face of Raven Crag, where rock climbers are busy.

At times the path is wide and of springy turf, at others it is wet nd rock strewn, but it is always downwards and after the steep limb up the gill it is a great relief on the legs. Harebells deck the verge and where the path eventually comes close to the fell wall, scabious and tormentil grow. Here, too, are several tall ash where a host of young blue tits perform acrobatics as they hunt for abundant prey.

The path continues down the road. Turn right and ahead lies the church and the lane to the left where the car has been parked.

O.S. Map NY324059
2 miles

Path at the end of the walk.

Waterfalls on Over Beck, west of Yewbarrow, Wast Water

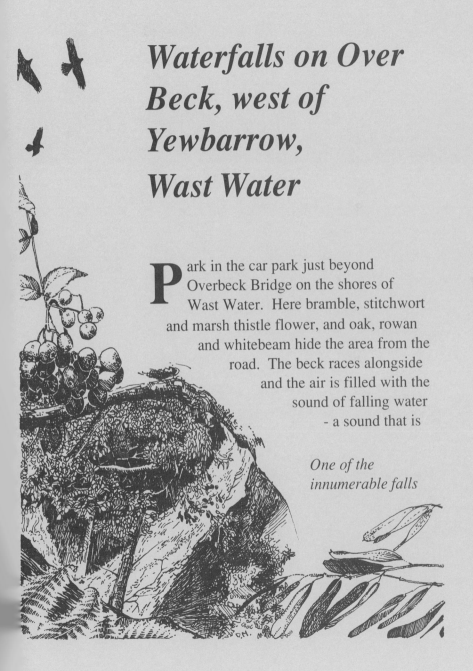

Park in the car park just beyond Overbeck Bridge on the shores of Wast Water. Here bramble, stitchwort and marsh thistle flower, and oak, rowan and whitebeam hide the area from the road. The beck races alongside and the air is filled with the sound of falling water - a sound that is

One of the innumerable falls

to accompany the walker throughout the day spent in the valley of Over Beck.

Follow the footpath close beside the mountain stream. Ahead graceful larches lean over the first of the many falls on this turbulent beck's headlong race to the lake. On the opposite bank cushions of heather luxuriate in the spray. Chaffinches and wrens flit through the branches of birch and rowan that line the small gorge, their songs unheard, drowned by the noise of the beck.

A huge boulder divides the Over Beck

The narrow track climbs the side of the gorge through bracken, tormentil and wood sage, to join the main footpath above. To the right the steep slopes of Yewbarrow soar upwards. Harebells line the path and sway gently in the light summer breeze. At the gate take the path that runs straight ahead into the bracken, keeping beside the surging water. Within a hundred yards the land on the left of the path drops steeply to the foaming Over. Ash, oak, elm, rowan, holly and birch clothe the ravine but are well scattered, allowing delightful views of innumerable falls. Large bunches of keys burden the ash trees and the rich red berries of the rowan glow warmly in the August sun. A jay flies low, its white rump revealing its presence.

The path climbs steadily and the sides of the beck are flatter and more open. There are few trees here to obscure the view of a series of turquoise pools and foaming falls. Clouds scud overhead and shadows chase the sunlight over the scree slopes of Dropping Crag, part of Yewbarrow's skirt.

Meadow pipits call from bracken and boulder, but there are far fewer birds now that so many have left for the seashore and migration. Look back regularly to Wast Water below. Sun and cloud create sparkling pools of light on the quiet stretch of dark water. Notice the mist lifting and then veiling the jagged tops of The Screes on the far side of the lake. Seemingly almost at one's feet lie the bright green cultivated fields of Bowderdale, wrested with such effort from the sometimes unsympathetic hand of nature, and enclosed by neat stone walls.

Continue along the path to where the beck surges around a long squat boulder. Its passageway is confined by a smaller rock projecting from the opposite bank. The water towers up at this constriction in its passage in frothing foam and then plummets down in a graceful fall. The berries on the rowan here are still green. Just before the footbridge a huge boulder, mid-stream, divides the Over Beck and two roaring torrents descend.

here are delightful views of innumerable falls

Below the wooden bridge the beck angrily negotiates a narrow canyon and tiny whirlpools form in small hollows at the side, sending the water back to rejoin the main flow once more. If the becks are not in spate cross the bridge, pass through a gap in the wall, turn right and pass through a gap in the wall ahead. Then strike uphill to find a wide, grassy path. This springy track swings across the fell, through bracken, until the side of Brimfell Beck is reached. This runs out of Low Tarn on High Fell and, if in spate, lives up to its name and is very difficult to cross. Brimfell is magnificent in full flow, raging through rowan, white topped for all its very considerable length. The current is swift and a giant - or the young with long legs - will be able to leap from boulder to boulder. For the not so agile or so young, it is better to return to the bridge and follow the trods that continue beside Over Beck.

Some scrambling is required but the glorious beck enchants and encourages the walker to continue onwards to see what lies ahead. Several wheatears remain on the fell and above circle raven, regularly disturbed by the more intrepid folk who have reached Yewbarrow's crown. Where the slopes are very wet, sundew carpet the ground, their red tipped leaves spread wide to catch their prey. The tall, delicate white flowers are in bloom.

Below, the beck descends in falls. Continue past these using sheep trods where possible to a large crag that appears to sit astride the beck, standing out boldly on the immediate skyline. From the top of the crag look ahead to Gosforth Crag Moss. Through this damp, grassy basin, surrounded by quiet fells, the Over Beck meanders lazily. Beside the crag the serene beck loses its peaceful ways. It swirls round a tiny island, covered with heather and hawkweed, in the middle of the lip at the top of a small precipice. It hurtles downwards in two white jets, unites in a pool and then drops down once more in an elegant fall. Heather, hard fern and moss line the sides of this delightful waterfall hidden below the large crag on the edge of the Moss.

Walk up the gentle, but wet, lower slopes of Yewbarrow to join a good track. Turn right and follow it as it runs below Long Crags and Dropping Crag. This is a grand way to return, walking into the sun, with Wast Water far below. To the west a tiny blue glimpse of sea sparkles in competition with the sparkling inland water. The footpath comes to a ladder stile over the wall. Turn right beyond and walk down the steep slope to the car park below.

O.S. Map NY167086
¹/₂ miles

Waterfalls in Mill Gill, Great Dodd, Vale of St. John

Hardheads and yarrow

C astle Rock is a familiar, friendly giant overlooking the foot of the Vale of St. John. Usually one is hurrying past it to somewhere else but today it becomes an intimate companion on the walk to the waterfalls in Mill Gill. The rock towers upwards and is much used by climbers and ravens. It inspired Sir Walter Scott, who used it as the setting for his poem 'The Bridal of Triermain', and by using one's imagination one can see its resemblance to a castle.

There is a large car parking area provided by North West Water at Legburthwaite, below the rock. On the O.S. map the car park is shown on the east side of the road but it actually lies on the west side. It is badly sign-posted and very easy to miss. From the car park follow the sign for Castle Rock along a footpath bordered with rose-bay willow-herb, angelica, ragwort and woundwort to a gate that opens onto the road. Cross the road to some steps and a gate to the fell beyond. Turn right and continue along a track that skirts a meadow full of summer flowers. Here, in great abundance, grow harebell, yarrow, hawkweed, hardhead, wild parsley, buttercup, betony, self-heal, tomentil, eyebright, clover and the lovely scabious. In scattered hawthorns about the fell blue tits keep up a constant chattering and on a bare branch of an oak the flash of a red tail reveals a common redstart. It sings its sweet happy song between short flights into the air after its prey.

The track continues and bracken on both sides replaces the lovely herbage. A young wren perches on a frond and sings its melodious song and then disappears, mouse-like, into the vegetation. Marsh thistle and spearwort brighten the damp flushes between the omnipresent fern. Just before a grey-painted barred gate with a big padlock take a path on the right that runs steeply uphill to the water race channelling water to the reservoir. Cross the race by a stile, a plank and another stile.

Water race

Walk upwards through the trees to a breach in the fell wall. A troop of coal tits restlessly move through the larches keeping up an incessant flock call. Above towers Castle Rock; it casts a dense shade for much of the year but at mid-day in August the sun is over-head and bright sun-beams pass through the trees to the soft green grass below.

Beyond the wall is a good view of the rock rearing into a blue sky.

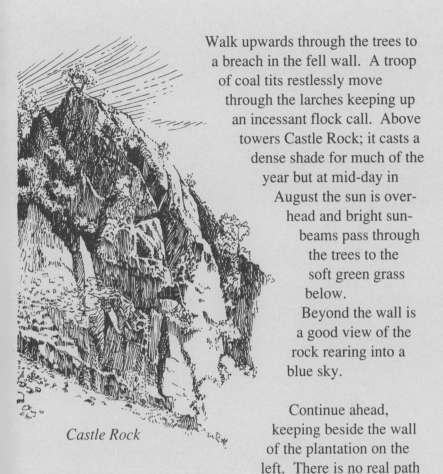

Castle Rock

Continue ahead, keeping beside the wall of the plantation on the left. There is no real path but several sheep trods show the easiest passage. Large boletus toadstools grow below the forest wall, a robin scolds from the branch of a larch and the air supports a vast population of crane flies. Beyond a man-made mound lies Mill Beck, chuckling on its way into the plantation. Cross over on some convenient rocks and walk with care upstream to see the foaming falls hidden in this narrow, perpendicular-sided ravine that slashes the northern skirt of Castle Rock.

The highest fall can be viewed only by leaving the sun-filled hollow and climbing upwards on some exceedingly slippery rocks. It descends in one long foaming jet. The beck races on around the base of a projecting crag and then plummets over water-blackened rocks into a pool. It surges through a deep gouge in a boulder set across it and plunges downwards once more into another pool before cascading on. The sheer sides of this lovely canyon support in crevices mosses, liverworts, wood sage, hawkbit, golden rod, male fern and foxgloves. Overhead lean ash, hazel, oak and hawthorn. A blackthorn bush laden with purple-blue sloes grows close to the water and rowan trees bear large clumps of vermillion berries.

It is hard to believe that this lovely isolated corner, with no trace of other human visitation, lies ten minutes from the road that leads to Grasmere and Keswick, where the streets are full of summer holiday-makers. Leave this fairy-like corner by a trod that runs upwards beneath an elegant larch and walk on along more trods until a small beck is reached. Away to the left a sparkling waterfall spills its lovely bounty in Ladknott Gill. Climb up beside the small beck to join a good track that crosses the fell, running between large stands of bracken. Turn right and follow the track upwards. It leads to the edge of another splendid ravine lined with birch, oak and rowan heavy with berries, beneath which flows Mill Beck in a series of lovely foaming falls and bright blue pools. Above, a buzzard circles lazily and effortlessly, its keening cry travelling across the mountain slopes, filling the air with menace.

Continue upwards, with care, beside the gill until the sides become less deep and then climb down to the edge of the pretty beck. Walk and scramble upwards, crossing from one side to the other in order to progress easily until, unobscured by dense vegetation, the beck is seen descending in more spectacular cascades and falls. On vegetation beside the splashing water a dozen or more meadow pipits call quietly as they feed. A sparrow-hawk planes just overhead and the pipits rise as one and fly off over the fell unpursued for once by the raptor.

Leave the beck and climb up the fellside, a long hot clamber on a lovely summer's day, to the cairn marking Little Dodd. From here the lovely charms of Lakeland lie revealed. Closest is High Rigg, with Tewet Tarn, a pool of blue, and the Castlerigg Stone Circle beyond. To the north and north-west the slopes of Blencathra and Skiddaw are purple with heather. The conifer-covered Dodd lies beyond. Further to the north-west lie Bassenthwaite Lake and The Bishop rock, starkly white on Barf, the Solway and the mountains of Scotland. To the west, above a corner of Derwent Water, lies Grisedale Pike. Grasmoor, Whiteless Pike, Scope End, Hindscarth, Robinson, Pillar and Great Gable stretch away to the south-west. One can see Scafell Pike, Bow Fell, and Crinkle Crags in the misty distance and Thirlmere darkly sparkling far below. To the south, beyond Watson's Dodd and Stybarrow Dodd, is Helvellyn, its summit and ridges crowded with walkers. Here on Great Dodd the writer and her companion are alone.

O.S. Map NY323197
*   NY325199*
3 miles

Waterfalls on Far Ruddy Beck, Crummock Water

The magnificent mountains around Crummock Water and Buttermere dramatically unfold as the approach is made from the west. In early October the lovely vista is just a silhouette, as mist veils crevice and outcrop. A gentle breeze, sufficient to rustle the ageing leaves on the trees, does little to lift the moisture-laden atmosphere. The dark green leaves of ash, sycamore and beech hardly allow light to penetrate but the sun streams through oak and birch whose leaves drift gently down. Their edges are touched with gold, highlighted as the day progresses by a strengthening sun which lifts the mist for a few hours. Along the roadside verges pink campion and herb robert are the last survivors of summer's plenty.

Leave the car in the car park in the village of Buttermere. The car park is a necessity that prevents the little hamlet from being strangled by this essential of modern life - but it is expensive. Walk on the left side of the Fish Hotel, towards the two lakes, following the signpost instructions. Overhead race a flock of house martins twittering excitedly as they prepare for their departure. Pied wagtails join in this noisy chatter as several birds, seemingly all tail and little body, dart overhead after the plenteous gnats that breed in the nearby Dubs and lakes. A sparrow-hawk, no doubt attracted by the prospect of an easy kill, flies menacingly low, but as the martins become aware of the intruder they leave their aerial acrobatics and begin to mob it.

An ash that appears to grow out of a rock

Pass through the gate beyond the hotel and then look for the gate and stile that gives access to a lane leading to Scale Bridge. The lane is hedged on one side and here a robin skulks and blue tits frolic in the mild mid-day air. Rose trees in the hedge are almost over burdened with a huge crop of scarlet hips. Blackthorn, whose blossoms were so welcome last spring, is now heavy with large round sloes. Elderberry, with stalks bare of berries, reveals the early depredations wrought upon it by a noisy flock of mistle thrushes. Rowan and honeysuckle both laden with a profusion of berries glow warmly in the sunshine and yet some large blossoms of honeysuckle still stretch up into the air above the hedge. Below this rich hedgerow harvest flower harebell and foxglove.

The lane comes to the edge of Buttermere Dubs, which is full of bright green weed through which trout dart. Occasionally they disturb the surface as they reach for flies. Figwort, heavily seeded, grows along the banks and a wren scolds angrily from the yellowing hazels and willows that line the river bank. Follow the track as it leads to the double-arched Scale Bridge, whose stones play host to the pretty spleenwort fern. Pass through the gate on the far side and turn right along a rough path that leads into the oak, ash and birch woodland that clothes the skirts of Red Pike. Look for the ash that appears to grow straight out of a huge rock, close beside a little stream racing down towards the Dubs. Along the edge of the Dubs more hazels grow, and between them small bushes of guelder rose, covered with clusters of fruit, each berry bright, glossy and brilliantly red like a shiny glass ball.

The stony path continues over open fell, cloaked with rich bronze-brown bracken that slopes up to dense birch cover above. Solitary ashes laden with bunches of papery keys and scrubby hawthorns glorious with deep red fruit add to the rich abundance of autumn. A red admiral dances across the path and pale fawn moths hurry across the slopes towards the birch. Cross Near Ruddy Beck on the soft pinky stones that line its bed and give it its name. Away to the right a heron rises lazily from the phragmites that colonises the shallow water at the head of Crummock. The bird alights again further from human disturbance. By now the lake is visible from the path and a small flock of red headed pochards can be seen regularly slipping below the placid waters after weeds and invertebrates. A single tufted duck idles near Holme Island, occasionally diving after its favourite weeds and insects.

A sheepfold on the right pinpoints Far Ruddy Beck. Turn up beside the tumbling water rather than crossing it by the small plank bridge. A

Plank bridge

small trod passing between dying bracken climbs the steep slopes among oaks and birches. Beneath these are numerous toadstools, puff balls and bracket fungi, the latter obtaining its food from fallen, decaying branches. Rowan berries scatter the path where it swings away from the beck. Here follow more trods that return to the side of the lush gorge. Where these become indistinct continue upwards over huge spongy mats of moss, soft to walk on, that carpet the ground between the widely scattered birches. The lemon-leaved trees, with the sun sloping through, turn this into a secluded fairyland.

View of three cascades through trees

Behind, more and more of the lake is revealed as the walker climbs higher. A flock of mistle thrushes blunder through several rowans, calling harshly and excitedly, no doubt responsible for the berries on the ground.

Continue climbing, lured on by the noise of falling water. A large mossy rock on the edge of the ravine acts as a natural viewing point overlooking the lovely waterfall on Far Ruddy Beck. Riotous vegetation obscures all but three of the cascades low down on the fall. These hurry in elegant lace curtains of water, foaming and spraying before descending into a small pool deep in a dark hollow at the bottom of the ravine. To see more of this lovely fall continue climbing upwards to where the verdant foliage no longer hides its glory. From here it is seen raging through the narrow gill, past lofty oaks festooned with polypody and lady fern, and plummeting in a long white-topped jet to a pool above the cascades. Climb upwards to the foot of another lovely waterfall on Far Ruddy Beck. The noisy beck rages down a very long rock slide at the base of which it swirls on either side of a squat flat boulder before dropping into a hollow floored with large pink rocks. In this hollow two feeder streams add their water to the beck before it descends the fall seen just before. This is the place for one's picnic and siesta before crossing the hollow and descending through knee-high bracken to the main path far below. The splendid views of Crummock Water give the walker plenty of excuses for pausing on this steepish descent.

).S. Map NY163168
miles

Waterfall, Warnscale Bottom, below Haystacks

There is a large parking area at Gatesgarth, east of Buttermere Lake, but get there early as it always seems full. Walk a hundred yards along the road in the direction of Honister Pass and then take the wide stony track on the right. This is well signposted and leads to Warnscale Bottom and the waterfalls.

The track is grassy in parts and skirts the base of Fleetwith Pike. Below Low Raven Crag on the left stands a white cross, a memorial to a lady who died in 1887. Continue along this pleasant, level track which in early October is bordered by bracken now a deep rich brown. This dying plant makes the

Path through the bracken

valley glow warmly in spite of the mist which hangs about the tops.

Follow the track as it comes close to a splendid stand of Scots pine and then continues parallel with a water-filled cut that helps to drain the low-lying ground of Warnscale Bottom. Meadow pipits remain on the fells and twitter cheerily as they flit ahead and then are quickly lost in the mist.

When a circular drystone sheep pen is reached leave the stony track and follow a grassy path that sweeps through the bracken to a footbridge over Warnscale Beck. Here among the grass tormentil and wild thyme flower. Ahead are the magnificent falls that enable the impetuous beck to reach the valley bottom.

Thyme and tormentil

The path, easy to follow, continues beside Warnscale Beck and then just before a spectacular fall it makes an acute right turn. From here the path climbs up the rocky slopes taking the walker away from the ravine through which the beck tumbles. Pause along the path and look up at the formidable heights, sides, screes and gullies of Haystacks and the fiercesome breach in the skyline through which roars Black Beck, white topped and angry. Wisps of mist, constantly moving, endow the amphitheatre of crags with a romantic and mysterious beauty.

112

Follow the well cairned path as it zig-zags upwards, past old quarry buildings, softened by time. When it swings away from the buildings, returning nearer to Warnscale Beck once more, walk to a small promontory and view the lovely beck in its deep canyon bordered by rowans rich in vermillion berries and red leaves. These contrast with the ash trees, still mainly green with just a few yellowing leaves. Below one's feet are clubmoss and alpine lady's mantle, with tiny yellow flowers. Ravens fly over the path emerging from the mist, then disappearing into it, as they exchange the steep slopes of Fleetwith Pike, on the far side of the beck, with Haystacks' craggy tops on the other.

The Warnscale plunges over a lip of rock at the top of this spectacular fall and slashes the mist with four graceful falls. Then it races furiously beneath a tall ash, foaming angrily as it drops in twin jets beneath the craggy sides of the pike. The water descends a smooth pavement of rock then cascades with droplets of water being tossed into the air. Still its fury is not spent and it plummets downhill once more in double cascades before uniting with the water of Black Beck.

The promontory overlooking the falls is an excellent viewpoint. Below lie the yellowing pastures around Gatesgarth Farm, the

View of the lake

autumnal grass brightening the valley with its warm colouring. Hedgerows border the pastures and beyond are the waters of Buttermere, sombre beneath lowering skies.

Leave the promontory and return to the path, heavily reinforced now, and continue climbing upwards. Below to the left lies another waterfall where the beck descends in a long foaming jet through a very narrow channel after leaving a rocky chaos. A dark cave runs back into the hillside at the top of the falling water.

Continue climbing. In places the path becomes very rocky but there is always a way even if, at times, it is tiring on the legs. More quarry buildings are passed on the right. To the left, down in its ravine, Warnscale Beck descends in another splendid water-fall, sending spray into the air as it hurtles downwards. As the sun begins to penetrate and then disperse the mist, the foam of the racing water changes from grey to white.

Convenient cairns mark the path as it swings on upwards above the quarry buildings and behind Green Crag. It arrives eventually at Blackbeck Tarn, from where issues the angry Black Beck seen earlier. Here there is a choice: to return beside the foaming Warnscale or to continue on to Innominate Tarn, Haystacks and Scarth Gap Pass. Both routes bring the walker back to the car park at Gatesgarth Farm.

O.S. Map NY201136
5 miles

Waterfall above Browney Gill, Great Langdale

Waterfall above Browney Gill, Great Langdale

It is always a pleasure to visit Great Langdale valley but it is a double pleasure in late October. Then the larches are clad in yellow and the leaves of the birches are pale gold; the mist hangs low over the fells until the sun penetrates and reveals each familiar peak clear-cut against the blue sky; the air seems washed clean and valleys, crags, ridges and tops appear close at hand; the pastures are a bright green and each meadow is full of livestock munching contentedly.

To reach the waterfall above Browney Gill leave the car at the well-sited car park just beyond the Old Dungeon Ghyll Hotel. Turn right at the entrance and walk to a farm gate immediately ahead. This gives access to a metalled track that leads through fields to Stool End Farm, owned by the National Trust. Take the much reinforced track that bears slightly to the left until a ladder stile is reached. After

Buttercup

116

walking over such a rocky path enjoy the next stretch which is wide, grassy and flat and leads deeper into Oxendale.

From here you might see the last hound trail of the season, as the hounds race down the slopes, across the path ahead and then up and over the wall. Follow the footpath signs and climb another ladder stile to a bridge over Oxendale Beck. Take a path that leads off to the right and then climbs upwards steeply, well marked with cairns but badly eroded. On either side only bugle and buttercup flower and the grass is withering, unlike the lush variety in the valley below. Some holly and birch maintain a precarious hold on the steep slope, the leaves of the latter a pale lemon.

This is a steep climb and many pauses are essential which give one time to enjoy the view. Far beyond the green Langdale Valley lies the Fairfield Horseshoe. Ahead are the familiar peaks of Harrison Stickle and Pike of Stickle with its long scree runnel seen in its entirety. To the left of the pikes is Hell Gill, a deep tree-lined trench above Whorneyside Force where the autumn tinted leaves can just be glimpsed. Beyond the gill lies Bow Fell, with mist occasionally obscuring its traditional shape and to the left of Bow Fell are the serrated tops of Crinkle Crags.

Ravens near Brown Howe

The path passes to the west of Brown Howe, entering a high, desolate valley where ravens congregate on the Howe. Regularly a pair circle upwards on the air currents calling harshly, and then acrobatically dive down to their viewpoint on the outcrops.

Follow the path through this valley and enjoy the more gentle climb. To the right, deep down, lies Browney Gill with the beck tumbling through it and its banks sparsely covered with trees. To the far right is a gully south-east of Great Knott. Down its vertical slopes a beck drops in long white, foaming jets of water before flowing sedately through the gill. Half way across the valley look for a change in soil colour from brown to red. The rocks too, change, and are a soft shade of pink. Both these effects are caused by haematite veins in the older rocks.

There is much bilberry here, but it is low growing, hugging the ground. Heather too is short but still in flower where it is sheltered. The path crosses a dry gill softened in outline by great patches of parsley fern that is just beginning to brown. It leads to a long spur of high ground between the dry gill just crossed and a very steep red-walled gill down which hurtles the waterfall. Long white streams of water race round impeding boulders, swirl to the right and then break into cascades. The water then rages round another impediment to fall in a long white jet into a brown-red pool. The water is clear and large boulders can be seen at the bottom. A few small rowans have taken root on the sides of the beck and heather and bilberry abound. The beck, after its impetuous jump, hurries on down to join the water that tumbles down the gully seen earlier, and together they form the beck that flows through Browney Gill.

After enjoying this delightful waterfall, continue climbing for a short distance to where the little beck wanders peacefully across the flat ground below the steep slopes of Pike of Blisco.

It crosses this marshy area after it has left Red Tarn which is fringed with sedge and common rush. A solitary tufted duck idles on the water and then it dives after aquatic weeds. For quite thirty minutes it keeps bobbing below the water and then popping up again, and then it tucks its bill into its wing and slumbers in the afternoon sun.

This is the place to find a sheltering rock, to slumber too, before making the descent into the valley where meadow pipits still frolic and the Langdale children are making guys for bonfire night.

O.S. Map NY262041 to NY264042
          NY265043

5 miles

Tufted duck on Red Tarn

Waterfalls above Ellers Beck, Maiden Moor, Derwent Water

The hedgerows and wooded fell slopes about Derwent Water blaze with yellows, bronzes, reds and golds as autumn sets its mark on this lovely vale. On the lake, in the warm sunshine of this late October morning, mallard and tufted duck display their plumage, resplendent after their moult. When the head of the lake is passed look for the elegant double-arched bridge across the River Derwent with signpost directions for Grange - but do not cross. There is space for two cars opposite the bridge and a hundred yards on is a larger parking area. There is parking space in Grange but if you use it this

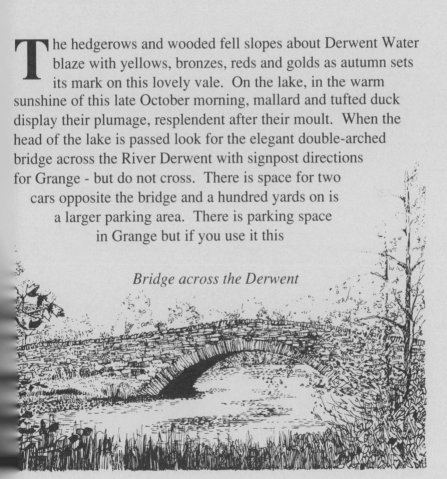

Bridge across the Derwent

might add to the traffic jam invariably associated with this little village. If you park by the gate that gives access to the walk you will not be able to enjoy the graceful bridge and the shops and facilities the village has to offer.

Walk through the village past Holy Trinity Church, where sheep graze beside the church wall, and continue past the school until a gate on the left, designated a footpath, is reached. Beyond the gate a narrow track leads diagonally to the left over pasture-land, with a scattering of beech, oak, holly, juniper, ash and gorse. The latter is covered with bright yellow blossoms and the beech and oak clothed in bronze and saffron. Robins sing their tender, sad winter song and a mistle thrush sits and enjoys the sun. One of the hollies is almost overloaded with berries, much to the delight of dozens of redwings that hasten through the tree and launch themselves in ecstatic flight over the slopes of Maiden Moor.

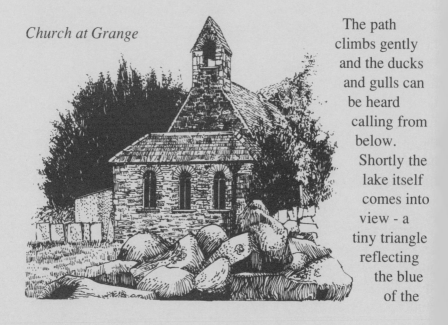

Church at Grange

The path climbs gently and the ducks and gulls can be heard calling from below. Shortly the lake itself comes into view - a tiny triangle reflecting the blue of the

October sky. The narrow path, swinging back to the right, leads to a gate in the fell wall and here herb robert, buttercup and tormentil flower. Keep to the scattered stones by the wall that borders High Close Wood, avoiding a very wet part of the track. Continue straight on along a springy turfed track that keeps to the left of a large water tank and comes to a gate in the wire fence. Beyond is a good track, part of the Allerdale Ramble, leading gently up the fell. From here the water-falls, almost hidden in their sheer-sided ravine, fill the air with the sound of falling water. Bear right through the dying bracken to the weir at the foot of the falls. Cross the beck and carefully climb up the far side of the canyon. Move down the sloping side until a huge ash that has fallen across the stream is reached. Sit on the trunk and look up to the lovely falls above.

Close up of middle jet

The Eller, divided by a huge boulder that sits athwart the precipitous lip, descends in two curtains of white lace beneath a guardian oak, covered with golden leaves. It unites to tumble on in foaming cascades past more oak, elm and birch aglow with golden foliage that catches the sunlight. Birch leaves continually drift downwards turning the sides of the beck to gold. The beck is then channelled down a narrow rock slide into a small surging pool surrounded with wood sorrel, golden saxifrage and foxglove leaves. It then races round tumbled rocks below the lovely ash which has fallen across the beck but remains rooted in the layered base of the gill. From the twin trunks of the parent tree, young branches have shot up towards the light and the leaves of these show no sign of autumn tints. Polypody fern and moss clothe the old trunks and ivy, heavy with flower buds, gracefully climbs one of the young sapling branches. Sturdy oaks border the rim of the gill and the steep slopes support bracken and heather covered with purple flowers.

Return to the foot of the fall and recross the hurrying Eller. Then strike up the grassy path that sweeps grandly through the bracken. In fifty yards it reaches a small knoll and from here there are magnificent views of the lake and also of the Jaws of Borrowdale, with misty silhouettes of the mountains beyond. Overhead flies a kestrel. Then a pair of ravens, croaking as they go, ascend to the rocky outcrops on the fell tops. What a glorious viewpoint for a perfect autumn day.

O.S. Map NY 245175
2 miles

Waterfall in Whelpside Gill, Thirlmere

Kestrel

Waterfall in Whelpside Gill, Thirlmere

T here is ample parking behind the church at Wythburn on the east shore of Thirlmere. On the last day of October it is a charming place to start one's walk to the falls in Comb Gill and the waterfall in Whelpside Gill. The needles of the larches are a pale gold, the leaves of young birches are a soft lemon and both contrast pleasingly with the green slate roof of the church and the dark mirror surface of the lake. Beyond the still waters are the grass-clad slopes, now straw coloured, around the Wythburn Beck.

A male kestrel sits on the church wall very still and rather hunched as it watches vigilantly for prey. Its rump and head are grey but its exquisitely patterned chestnut back blends well with the dying bracken below the wall. A robin 'tics' angrily from a very tall cypress in the churchyard, disturbed by either the kestrel or human intruders.

Leave the car park by a kissing gate in the north-east corner and continue up through the conifers following a stony track. To the left, beyond an ancient drystone wall, is the racing water of the beck that flows through Comb Gill. It noisily negotiates boulders and drops in its bed, a brilliant white beneath the dark-needled spruce trees that stretch away to the north. A coal tit flits across the path and alights on a conifer twig, causing it to sway across the frothing water. Soft parchment-brown needles blow across one's face as a slight breeze moves the branches overhead.

Cross the permissive path that traverses the plantation and follow the signpost direction for Helvellyn. This is another rocky path flanked by tall cypresses that resound to the gentle chatter of goldcrests. A gate gives access to the open fell, now a rich brown expanse of dead bracken, and through this the track ascends in two large zig-zags, by-passing the serious erosion that has occurred on this popular walk. Look across the lake to where the waterfalls in the Wythburn valley can be seen slashing the hillside in a long white streak of white. The path comes close to a wall on the left that borders more conifers and from these there is a constant twitter of coal tits.

View of Combe Gill

127

The wall and trees cease and the falls that race pell-mell through Comb Gill, beneath Comb Crag, lie ahead. The white streams drop tempestuously through the bare slopes of this sheltered hollow in a series of narrow, foam-topped cascades until they are lost to sight in the plantation. Turn left, leaving the main track, and strike across the boulder-strewn slopes of Middle Tongue where the grass is bleached. Sphagnum moss, red topped, hosts a mass of water and buttercup and herb robert still flower. A large stride takes one across each of several small tributaries of Comb Beck, even if they are in spate. Within a hundred yards the walker reaches the path that overlooks the magnificent waterfall below the scree and rocky slopes of Whelp Side.

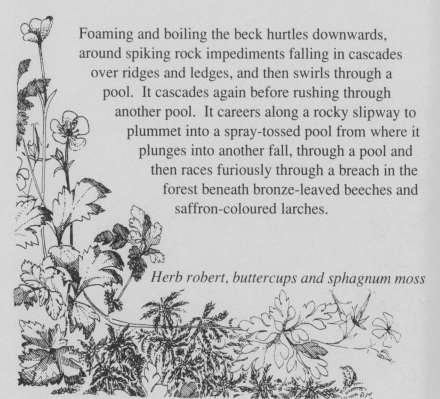

Foaming and boiling the beck hurtles downwards, around spiking rock impediments falling in cascades over ridges and ledges, and then swirls through a pool. It cascades again before rushing through another pool. It careers along a rocky slipway to plummet into a spray-tossed pool from where it plunges into another fall, through a pool and then races furiously through a breach in the forest beneath bronze-leaved beeches and saffron-coloured larches.

Herb robert, buttercups and sphagnum moss

Descend through the secluded gill, keeping between the beck and the wall. Here is a gentle quietness with no eroded paths or trace of other members of the human race. Leave the gill by a gate in the wall and follow an indistinct path beneath larches which leads to a stile over an old wire fench. The little track continues downwards. Now the two becks, Comb and Whelp, have come closer together and their merry gurglings accompany one all the way. When a barrier of young larch impedes the path, walk through the trees for twenty yards or so to the permissive path crossed earlier. Turn left and walk to a gate and stile where the signpost directs the walker downhill to Wythburn Church.

.S. Map NY331139

/2 miles

Waterfalls in Wray Gill, Grasmere

C an anywhere be more glorious than Grasmere in
November, when every tree is a riot of colour, the
meadows about the village are bright green, the lake is the
blue of the sky it is reflecting, the sun is very bright even though
low in the sky and the mountains all around are covered in deep
snow? All is idyllic. Viewed from the paths to Wray Gill and
from much of the gill itself, Grasmere's beauty is enhanced
because the eye can take in all the splendour in a glance.

Park in the car park just beyond the Tourist Information Office.
Turn left along the road to Red Bank and take the second gate on
the right after the bridge. This gives access to a walled path
signposted to Langdale. After an initial rockiness, the path is
easy to walk. Polypody fern, wood sorrel leaves, climbing
corydalis in bloom, and brambles still heavy with fruit abound.
On a larch over the wall a nuthatch searches for insects, its upper
parts slate-grey and its eye-stripe black. From nearby a loud
clear whistle reveals another, zig-zagging up a trunk.

The walled path is gated at its end and then a waymarked path
crosses parkland to an opening in the fell wall. Beyond the wall
turn right and follow a path across the fell, with the lowest of the
beck's falls beckoning through the trees.

Buttercups flower but the ash has lost its leaves and its huge
bunches of key-shaped seeds are quite brown. The path climbs

View of the lake and polypody

slowly towards the noise of the tumbling water. It passes under a fallen conifer and past a Norway spruce with long, thin, brown cones haunted by goldcrests. Continue to the edge of the gill to where white water topples from a steep, rocky slipway and then spreads out like white lace beneath a hawthorn tree with green leaves and rich red berries. Overhead fly a pair of crows.

Climb down the easy slopes to the edge of the water and then scramble through the gill where ferns, moss, heather and holly all thrive in the sheltered, grassy, secluded ravine.

Soon the foot of the next fall is reached. Here the water drops in one long white stream, to divide into two frothing jets that send spray in all directions then reunite beneath a screen of holly. Here grow wood sage, bramble and foxgloves.

Scramble up the side and out of the ravine and follow a track through the dying bracken to a ladder stile. Stand atop the stile and enjoy the parkland below and an extensive view of the lake sparkling and clear beyond.

Walk along more sheep tracks to the side of the beck again to a magnificent waterfall above. Dozens of tiny cascades slip over small ledges as the lively beck, white-topped, dances down a steep slope between holly and juniper. Several protruding boulders divide the water into two long water slides which come together in a deep pool. The beck races along another rocky slipway and then tumbles down in more foaming falls.

Above are jagged rocks, gnarled oaks and larches laden with cones. Beneath the oaks grow heather and glossy-leaved ivy. Now the faint path is snowy underfoot and a little slippery but continue climbing the gill, keeping close to the water's edge so that none of the beck's tantrums or triumphs are missed.

Follow the indistinct track, skirting a flank of Silver How, and take a last look at the lovely view behind. Ahead lies perhaps the most spectacular waterfall, lying deep in a cleft that itself is tucked into a fold of this pleasant mountain. The water comes down in a long, wide ribbon of white water raging over its

Spectacular waterfalls

133

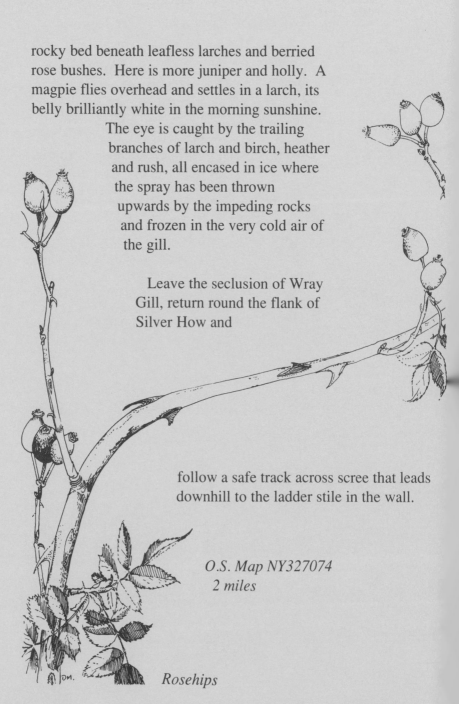

rocky bed beneath leafless larches and berried
rose bushes. Here is more juniper and holly. A
magpie flies overhead and settles in a larch, its
belly brilliantly white in the morning sunshine.
The eye is caught by the trailing
branches of larch and birch, heather
and rush, all encased in ice where
the spray has been thrown
upwards by the impeding rocks
and frozen in the very cold air of
the gill.

Leave the seclusion of Wray
Gill, return round the flank of
Silver How and

follow a safe track across scree that leads
downhill to the ladder stile in the wall.

O.S. Map NY327074
2 miles

Rosehips

Waterfalls between Helvellyn Screes and Whelp Side, Thirlmere

Redpoll and larch

Waterfalls between Helvellyn Screes and Whelp Side, Thirlmere

The daylight hours in early December are few and walks to waterfalls have to be timed carefully. The day chosen could be one of sunshine and showers so the walk from Wythburn Church to the waterfalls directly below Helvellyn is a very suitable choice. It is not too long; most of the way is easy walking and the route is all one's own as most of the other walkers seem to be making for the tops.

Leave the car behind the little church that stands solitary, without a settlement around it, towards the south end of the reservoir. The larches that have obscured much of the view all summer have lost their leaves and now, after a wet autumn, one can see the high level of the lake, the bleached shoreline of summer submerged. Beyond the lake wisps of mist hang low over the Wythburn Fells and Ullscarf.

Take the gate that leads to Helvellyn and then turn right, clambering upwards over a worn path that passes below cypresses and larches. The latter are laden with cones and a flock of redpoll search acrobatically and industriously for food. A hundred yards up the slope is a stile and a signpost that stands on the edge of a permissive path. Climb the stile and walk northwards along the path. This is a forest ride and is carpeted with russet-coloured larch needles and beech leaves. These glow warmly as the low sun slants through the trees.

Below, to the left, is a glorious view of the lake, its glassy surface reflecting the trees on the western shore, darkly and sombrely because of the black rain clouds above. A short way beyond the stile two pretty becks flow under the path after tumbling white-topped through the trees, hastening urgently to the lake below. Here a flock of coal tits meticulously seeks for insects in the lower branches of larch and birch. As one bird flits from branch to branch, a shower of sparkling raindrops is dislodged by its tiny weight.

A red squirrel also is hunting for food low in the trees and when disturbed scrambles rapidly up the trunk of a larch. It pauses and looks down on the intruders and, feeling insecure,

Second bridge over the beck

scrambles higher up. Then, to be quite safe, it leaps across to another tree, this time a pine where it is quickly lost among the dense foliage.

At the end of this section of the plantation a stile gives access to a reinforced path that crosses the base of a gill before entering another part of the forest below Helvellyn Screes. Through this gap in the rows of trees tumble two becks crossed by wooden bridges. The second bridge gives a charming view of one of the becks as it races in continuous falls down the steep slope into the lake. The waterfalls on this beck are the object of the walk. Keeping to the right side of the stream climb up the rough fell. There are sheep tracks and indistinct paths to follow that bring the walker to a wire mesh fence.

Pause here and look up the gill to where Helvellyn is shrouded in thick mist. A wide, white cascade of water leaping out of the mist is all that can be seen. Climbers follow the beck past old mine workings to its source and then ascend the fell above, reaching the top of this popular peak by the shortest route.

The beck swings to the left and then, impeded by a large boulder, leaps in two dramatic foam-topped falls that spread out in a curtain before tumbling into a small pool. Then the beck

Ferns, moss and rosehips

idles through a delightful, secluded rock cutting flanked by rowan, ash and holly. A large juniper bush clings to the steep side of the cleft and several coal tits work through the foliage. Their feathers are very wet and very black and this accentuates the white of their cheeks, making them easy to see. Below in the gill are ferns, heather, bracken, and mosses, all still green with only small touches of autumn colourings, and rose hips, bright scarlet, brighten a dark recess. The small flat areas of grass must make tempting sunbeds in the summer.

Stand by the large rowan on the edge of the secluded cleft and look down the breach in the conifers to the glass-like lake below. On the other side of the water a wide path can be seen winding its way towards Harrop Tarn, and the falls below the tarn are pristine white among the dark green pines.

O.S. Map NY324148
2¹/₂ miles

Waterfall in Blindtarn Gill, Silver How, Grasmere

S ilver How lies to the west of Grasmere. At the base of this lovely fell are fine oaks, birches, beeches and conifers. Extensive areas of juniper spread over the fell above the trees and then the grassy top is clothed with bracken among the rocky outcrops. Down Silver How's slopes tumble lively becks which pass through Meg's Gill, Wray Gill and Blindtarn Gill. In each gill are spectacular falls. Meg's was visited in high summer (see Walk 19), Wray's in late autumn (Walk 28) and the waterfall in Blindtarn Gill is the object of this walk, in the week before Christmas.

Leave the car in the car park in Easedale Road. From here Fairfield can be seen, its head in mist which occasionally drifts away leaving the peak bathed in sunshine. Turn right from the car park, walking along the road away from the village. The hedgerow hawthorns are laden with berries and the gutters are littered with fallen beech leaves. Ignore the right turn that leads to the A591 and when the road swings to the right for Far Easedale, leave it and cross a sturdy footbridge over Easedale Beck into winter woodland.

Walk through the trees and a gate to a track that runs beside the fast flowing beck. Here mistle thrushes, when disturbed, fly off to distant trees and young rooks sit in the leafless ashes beside the beck. Ahead lies the huge white waterfall, dropping down Sourmilk Gill, visited in Book One.

Soon the track is walled on the left and then a signpost directs the walker to Blindtarn Moss, through a gate. The path is not easy to follow in places so, keeping a drystone wall to the right, head for a gap in the wall ahead. This leads into a wooded area where a pair of mallards are feeding under the oaks. The path lies through another gap in another wall and passes a cottage. Here is a gate with an awkward catch.

After the gate strike across the rough fell, with its clumps of juncus and reed, towards the raging beck. Juniper and holly line its banks and pigeons fly from the trees on the slopes beyond. Higher, the beck cascades, white-topped, beneath oak, rowan, ash, berried holly and juniper. Above the cascades lies the waterfall.

It descends in a wide wall of white water to be divided by a large rock into two smaller streams. Then it is parted once more by huge projections so that it tumbles on down in three jets of racing water. These drop into a swirling pool before hurrying downhill. Leaning over this lovely fall in its isolated hollow are hawthorn, willow and birch with minute catkins. Here too grows a huge holly with large sprays of vermillion berries and all around are clumps of juniper.

This is a glorious, secluded cleft in which to idle, out of the wind yet bathed in

Mallards feeding under the oak

Cascades through the trees

sunlight. When you can drag yourself away climb up the grassy sides of the gill to a path above which passes more juniper bushes. These are covered in berries, some of which are grey-green and others a rich purple. A host of coal tits flits through these delicately needled but hardy shrubs. The white of the birds' cheeks and nape contrasts sharply with the blackness of their heads and quickly reveals their whereabouts.

The path continues upwards and, away to the right, can be heard the noise of the turbulent beck as it cascades once more. Hardy sheep abound on the upper slopes and a large ram takes an aggressive step forward, anxious for its ewes. The path, now even more indistinct, begins to ascend Swinescar Hause (keeping well away from Blindtarn Moss, which lies to the right and is a very wet area). But the daylight hours are short in December and the mist comes down early, so one cannot continue along this way.

Instead, return along the path past the Moss and through the juniper, which is still alive with the chatter of coal tits. A yellow hammer, disturbed, flies off across the top of the bushes, showing its bright yellow underparts.

Ram and ewes

Follow the main path down
the fell, leaving the waterfall away to
the left. Ahead are glorious views of
Grasmere and the high fells around. On the walk back along the
lane, jays call raucously from oaks behind Allen Bank.

O.S. Map NY322079
3 miles